Modern

Concurrency

in Swift

By Marin Todorov

Modern Concurrency in Swift

By Marin Todorov

ISBN: 978-1-950325-81-8

Table of Contents

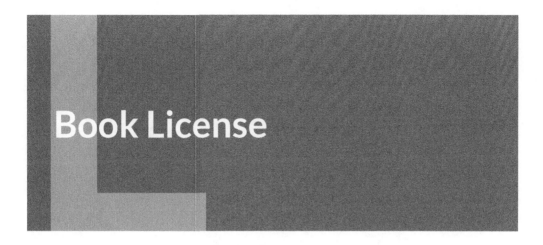

Book License

By purchasing *Modern Concurrency in Swift*, you have the following license:

- You are allowed to use and/or modify the source code in *Modern Concurrency in Swift* in as many apps as you want, with no attribution required.

- You are allowed to use and/or modify all art, images and designs that are included in *Modern Concurrency in Swift* in as many apps as you want, but must include this attribution line somewhere inside your app: "Artwork/images/designs: from *Modern Concurrency in Swift*, available at www.kodeco.com".

- The source code included in *Modern Concurrency in Swift* is for your personal use only. You are NOT allowed to distribute or sell the source code in *Modern Concurrency in Swift* without prior authorization.

- This book is for your personal use only. You are NOT allowed to sell this book without prior authorization, or distribute it to friends, coworkers or students; they would need to purchase their own copies.

Before You Begin

This section tells you a few things you need to know before you get started, such as what you'll need for hardware and software, where to find the project files for this book, and more.

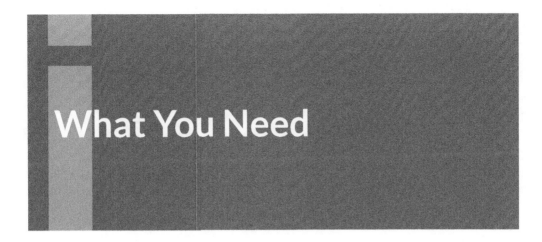

What You Need

To follow along with this book, you'll need the following:

- A Mac running **macOS Ventura (13.0)** or later. Monterey should work, but this book was written and tested on macOS Monterey, so your mileage may vary.

- **Xcode 14 or later**. Xcode is the main development tool for iOS. You'll need Xcode 14 or newer for the tasks in this book. If you're using Xcode 13.2 and above, the new async/await syntax and the rest of the modern concurrency features will work starting with iOS 13 / macOS 10.15 SDK (or later). If you're using an older version of Xcode 13, you'll only get modern concurrency support when targeting iOS 15 / macOS 12. You can download the latest version of Xcode from Apple's developer site (https://apple.co/2asi58y)

- **An intermediate level of Swift**. Concurrency in general is a relatively advanced topic, so you need to have at least an intermediate-level knowledge of Swift and its existing concurrency features. This book won't teach pre-Swift 5.5 Concurrency features such as Grand Central Dispatch, but you should still be able to follow the contents of this book, even if you're not entirely proficient with them.

This book does **not** require a physical device. However, you might want to try some of the advanced concurrency features on a real device, so you can truly feel how it works in "the real world".

Book Source Code & Forums

Where to Download the Materials for This Book

The materials for this book can be cloned or downloaded from the GitHub book materials repository:

- https://github.com/kodecocodes/mcon-materials/tree/editions/2.0

Forums

We've also set up an official forum for the book at https://forums.kodeco.com/c/books/modern-concurrency-in-swift. This is a great place to ask questions about the book or to submit any errors you may find.

"Dedicated to my daughter and family. Warm thanks to
everyone on the extended team that made this book possible."

— *Marin Todorov*

About the Authors

Marin Todorov is a developer, speaker and author. He works for high-profile clients, most often doing Swift development.Besides crafting code, he enjoys blogging, writing books, teaching and speaking. He sometimes open-sources his code.More about Marin at: underplot.com

About the Editors

Rich Turton is a tech editor for this book. He's been developing apps for Apple platforms since before it was cool. He lives in the UK with his wife, daughters and terrible cat.

Felipe Laso Marsetti is a tech editor for this book. He's a Technical Lead working at Lextech Global Services. In his spare time, Felipe enjoys learning new languages and frameworks, playing violin and guitar, cooking and also video games. You can follow him on Twitter as @iFeliLM (https://twitter.com/iFeliLM).

Shai Mishali is the final pass editor on this book. He's an experienced, award-winning iOS specialist, an international speaker and a highly active open-source contributor and maintainer on several high-profile projects. He works on the RxSwift Community and RxSwift projects, but also releases many open-source endeavors around Combine such as CombineCocoa, RxCombine and more. As an avid enthusiast of hackathons, Shai took first place at BattleHack Tel-Aviv 2014, BattleHack World Finals San Jose 2014 and Ford's Developer Challenge Tel-Aviv 2015. You can find him on GitHub (https://github.com/freak4pc) and Twitter as @freak4pc (https://twitter.com/freak4pc).

Acknowledgments

We would like to thank Audrey Tam, Marin Benčević and Piotr Fulmanski for their help in reviewing portions of this book and providing their feedback.

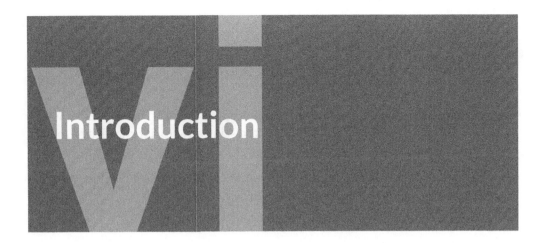

Introduction

Welcome to *Modern Concurrency in Swift*, the book that walks you through the amazing concurrency APIs introduced by Apple in Swift 5.5.

Swift is a powerful, all-purpose programming language that's currently expanding beyond Apple's platforms (like iOS, macOS, tvOS and so on) and into new platforms like Linux, Windows, and more.

To help the language take on a whole new set of tasks, Swift 5.5 introduced a modern concurrency model with a native syntax for asynchronous operations and tighter integration between the concurrent APIs, the compiler and runtime.

Most of the books from Kodeco are "By Tutorials". Since this book targets developers who already have intermediate/advanced Swift skills, however, we skipped that part of the book title.

The book chapters consist of a healthy mix of theory sections that introduce new concepts and APIs, and step-by-step tutorials. By the time you're done working through all the projects, Swift's concurrency model won't hold any secrets for you!

Take a deep breath and enjoy the ride!

How to read this book

Most of this book's chapters build from one concept to the next. We suggest reading it chapter-by-chapter to make sure you aren't missing any crucial knowledge you need for any of the advanced chapters.

However, the chapters are also mostly self-contained, so if you feel comfortable with one of the topics, feel free to skip ahead to the next topic in the list.

Section I: Modern Concurrency in Swift

Chapter 1: Why Modern Swift Concurrency?

By Marin Todorov

The last time Apple made a big deal about an asynchronous framework was when **Grand Central Dispatch (GCD)** came out, along with Mac OS X Snow Leopard, in 2009.

While GCD helped Swift launch in 2014 with support for concurrency and asynchrony from day one, that support wasn't native — it was designed around the needs and abilities of Objective-C. Swift just "borrowed" that concurrency until it had its own mechanism, designed specifically for the language.

All that changed with Swift 5.5, which introduced a new, native model for writing asynchronous, concurrent code.

The new **concurrency model** provides everything you need to write safe and performant programs in Swift, including:

- A new, native syntax for running asynchronous operations in a structured way.

- A bundle of standard APIs to design asynchronous and concurrent code.

- Low-level changes in the `libdispatch` framework, which make all the high-level changes integrate directly into the operating system.

- A new level of compiler support for creating safe, concurrent code.

Swift 5.5 introduced new language syntax and APIs to support these features. In your apps, besides using a recent Swift version, you also need to target certain platform versions:

- If you're using Xcode 13.2 or newer, it will bundle the new concurrency runtime with your app so you can target iOS 13 and macOS 10.15 (for native apps).

- In case you're on Xcode 13.0 or Xcode 13.1, you'll have to target iOS 15 or macOS 12 at a minimum. Consider updating to Xcode 14 or above to be able to make use of the newest features.

In the first chapter of the book, you'll review the new concurrency support in Swift and see how it fares compared to older APIs. Later, in the practical part of the chapter, you'll work on a real-life project by trying out the async/await syntax and adding some cool asynchronous error-handling.

Understanding Asynchronous and Concurrent Code

Most code runs the same way you see it written in your code editor: from top to bottom, starting at the beginning of your function and progressing line-by-line to the end.

This makes it easy to determine when any given code line executes — it simply follows the one before it. The same is true for function calls: When your code runs **synchronously**, the execution happens sequentially.

In a synchronous context, code runs in one **execution thread** on a single CPU core. You can imagine synchronous functions as cars on a single-lane road, each driving behind the one in front of it. Even if one vehicle has a higher priority, like an ambulance on duty, it cannot "jump over" the rest of the traffic and drive faster.

On the other hand, iOS apps and Cocoa-based macOS apps are inherently **asynchronous**.

Asynchronous execution allows different pieces of the program to run in any order on one thread — and, sometimes, *at the same time* on multiple threads, depending on many different events like user input, network connections and more.

In an asynchronous context, it's hard to tell the *exact order* in which functions run, especially when several asynchronous functions need to use the same thread. Just like driving on a road where you have stoplights and places where traffic needs to yield, functions must sometimes wait until it's their turn to continue, or even stop until they get a green light to proceed.

One example of an asynchronous call is making a network request and providing a completion closure to run when the web server responds. While waiting to run the completion callback, the app uses the time to do other chores.

execution

To intentionally run parts of your program **in parallel**, you use **concurrent** APIs. Some APIs support executing a fixed number of tasks at the same time; others start a concurrent group and allow an arbitrary number of concurrent tasks.

This could also cause some concurrency-related problems. For example, different parts of the program might block each other's execution, or you might encounter the much-loathed **data-races**, where two or more functions simultaneously access the same variable, crashing the app as a result.

However, when used with care, concurrency can help your program run faster by executing different functions simultaneously on multiple CPU cores, the same way careful drivers can move much faster on a multi-lane freeway.

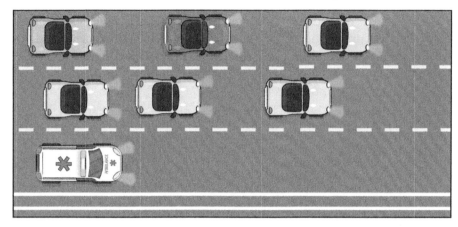

Multiple lanes allow faster cars to go around slower vehicles. Even more importantly, you can keep the emergency lane free for high-priority vehicles, like ambulances or firetrucks.

Similarly, when executing code, high-priority tasks can "jump" the queue before lower-priority tasks, so you avoid blocking the main thread and keep it free for critical updates to the UI.

A real use-case for this is a photo browsing app that needs to download a group of images from a web server *at the same time*, scale them down to thumbnail size and store them in a cache.

While asynchrony and concurrency both sound great, you might ask yourself: "Why did Swift need a *new* concurrency model?". That's a fair question and you'll review the pre-Swift 5.5 concurrency options and learn what's different about the new async/await model in the next section.

Reviewing the Existing Concurrency Options

Pre-Swift 5.5, you used GCD to run asynchronous code via dispatch queues — an abstraction over threads. You also used older APIs that are 'closer to the metal', like `Operation`, `Thread` or even interacting with the C-based `pthread` library directly.

> **Note**: You won't use GCD in this book because the new Swift concurrency APIs have replaced it. If you're curious, read Apple's GCD documentation: Dispatch documentation (https://apple.co/3tOlEuO).

Those APIs all use the same foundation: **POSIX threads**, a standardized execution model that doesn't rely on any given programming language. Each execution flow is a **thread**, and multiple threads might overlap and run at the same time, similarly to the multi-lane car example presented above.

Thread wrappers like `Operation` and `Thread` require you to **manually manage** execution. In other words, you're responsible for creating and destroying threads, deciding the order of execution for concurrent jobs and synchronizing shared data across threads. This is error-prone and tedious work.

GCD's queue-based model worked well. However, it was also prone to issues, like:

- **Thread explosion**: Creating too many concurrent threads requires constantly switching between active threads. This ultimately *slows down* your app instead of making it go faster.

- **Priority inversion**: When arbitrary, low-priority tasks block the execution of high-priority tasks waiting in the same queue.

- **Lack of execution hierarchy**: Asynchronous code blocks lacked an execution hierarchy, meaning each task was managed independently. This made it difficult to cancel or access running tasks. It also made it complicated for a task to return a result to its caller.

To address these shortcomings, Swift 5.5 introduced a brand-new concurrency model. Next, you'll see what modern concurrency in Swift is all about!

Introducing the Modern Swift Concurrency Model

The new concurrency model is tightly integrated with the language syntax, the Swift runtime and Xcode. It abstracts away the notion of threads for the developer. Its key new features include:

1. A black-box cooperative thread pool.

2. async/await syntax.

3. Structured concurrency.

4. Context-aware code compilation.

With this high-level overview behind you, you'll now take a deeper look at each of these features.

1. A Cooperative Thread Pool

The new model transparently manages a pool of threads to ensure it doesn't exceed the number of CPU cores available. This way, the runtime doesn't need to create and destroy threads or constantly perform expensive thread switching. Instead, your code can suspend and, later on, resume very quickly on any of the available threads in the pool.

2. async/await Syntax

Swift's new async/await syntax lets the compiler and the runtime know that a piece of code might suspend and resume execution one or more times in the future. The runtime handles this for you seamlessly, so you don't have to worry about threads and cores.

As a wonderful bonus, the new language syntax often removes the need to weakly or strongly capture self or other variables because you don't need to use escaping closures as callbacks.

3. Structured Concurrency

Each asynchronous task is now part of a hierarchy, with a parent task and a given priority of execution. This hierarchy allows the runtime to cancel all child tasks when a parent is canceled. Furthermore, it allows the runtime to *wait* for all children to complete before the parent completes. It's a tight ship all around.

This hierarchy provides a huge advantage and a more obvious outcome, where high-priority tasks will run before any low-priority tasks in the hierarchy.

4. Context-aware Code Compilation

The compiler keeps track of whether a given piece of code *could* run asynchronously. If so, it won't let you write potentially unsafe code, like mutating shared state.

This high level of compiler awareness enables elaborate new features like **actors**, which differentiate between synchronous and asynchronous access to their state at compile time and protects against inadvertently corrupting data by making it harder to write unsafe code.

With all those advantages in mind, you'll move on to writing some code with the new concurrency features right away and see how it feels for yourself!

Running the Book Server

Throughout the rest of this chapter, you'll create a fully-fledged stock trading app with live price monitoring called **LittleJohn**.

You'll work through the code at a *quick pace*, with a somewhat brief explanation of the APIs. Enjoy the process and don't worry about the mechanics right now. You'll go into the nitty-gritty details at length in the coming chapters.

First things first: Most of the projects in this book need access to a web API to fetch JSON data, download images and more. The book comes with its own server app, called the **book server** for short, that you need to run in the background at all times while working through the chapters.

Open your Mac's Terminal app and navigate to the **00-book-server** folder in the book materials repository. Start the app by entering:

```
swift run
```

The first time you run the server, it will download a few dependencies and build them — which might take a minute or two. You'll know the server is up and running when you see the following message:

```
[ NOTICE ] Server starting on http://127.0.0.1:8080
```

To double-check that you can access the server, launch your favorite web browser and open the following address: http://localhost:8080/hello (http://localhost:8080/hello).

This contacts the book server running on your computer, which will respond with the current date:

Later, when you've finished working on a given project and want to stop the server, switch to your Terminal window and press **Control-C** to end the server process.

> **Note**: The server itself is a Swift package using the Vapor framework, but this book won't cover that code. If you're curious, you're welcome to open it in Xcode and read through it. Additionally, you can learn all about using Vapor by working through Server-Side Swift with Vapor (https://www.kodeco.com/books/server-side-swift-with-vapor).

Getting Started with LittleJohn

As with all projects in this book, LittleJohn's SwiftUI views, navigation, and data model are already wired up and ready for you. It's a simple ticker app that displays selected "stock prices" live:

> **Note**: The server sends random numbers to the app. Don't read anything into any upward or downward trends of these fictitious prices!

As mentioned earlier, simply *go with the flow* in this chapter and enjoy working on the app. You'll revisit everything you do here in later chapters, where you'll learn about all the APIs in greater detail.

The first thing you need to do is to add some asynchronous code to the main app screen.

Introducing async/await

As your first task, you'll add a function to the app's model that fetches a list of available stocks from the web server in JSON format. That's a very common task in iOS programming, so it's a fitting first step.

Open the starter version of LittleJohn in this chapter's materials, under **projects/starter**. Then, open **LittleJohnModel.swift** and add a new method inside LittleJohnModel:

```
func availableSymbols() async throws -> [String] {
  guard let url = URL(string: "http://localhost:8080/littlejohn/
symbols")
  else {
    throw "The URL could not be created."
  }
}
```

Let's look at the some of the key features of modern concurrency used in the code above.

The async keyword in the method's definition lets the compiler know that the code runs in an asynchronous context. In other words, it says that the code might suspend and resume at will. Also, regardless of how long the method takes to complete, it ultimately returns a value (or throws) much like a synchronous method does.

> **Note**: The starter projects in this book contain an extension on String so you can throw strings for brevity instead of creating custom error types.

Next, at the bottom of the new availableSymbols() method, add the code below to call URLSession and fetch data from the book server:

```
let (data, response) = try await URLSession.shared.data(from:
url)
```

Calling the async method URLSession.data(from:delegate:) suspends availableSymbols() and resumes it when it gets the data back from the server:

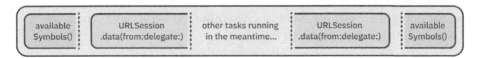

Using await gives the runtime a **suspension point**: a place to *pause* your method, consider if there are other tasks to run first and then continue running your code.

It's *so neat* that you make an asynchronous call but never have to worry about threads or passing closures around!

Next, you need to verify the server response and return the fetched data. Append this code to complete your method:

```
guard (response as? HTTPURLResponse)?.statusCode == 200 else {
  throw "The server responded with an error."
}

return try JSONDecoder().decode([String].self, from: data)
```

First, you check that the response code is 200. In server language, this means a successful **OK** response. Then, you try to decode the response data as a list of Strings. If that succeeds, you return the result.

You'll learn about async/await in greater detail in Chapter 2, "Getting Started With async/await".

> **Note**: Web servers can respond with a myriad of status codes; this book won't cover them all. Check out this list if you want to know more: HTTP status codes (https://bit.ly/2Yz12ww).

Using async/await in SwiftUI

Press **Command-B** to compile the project and verify you correctly added all the code so far, but don't run it just yet. Next, open **SymbolListView.swift**, where you'll find the SwiftUI code for the symbol list screen.

The essential part here is the ForEach that displays the symbols in a list onscreen. You need to call LittleJohnModel.availableSymbols(), which you just created, and assign its result to SymbolListView.symbols to get everything to work together.

Inside SymbolListView.body, find the .padding(.horizontal) view modifier. Add the following code immediately below it:

```
.onAppear {
  try await model.availableSymbols()
}
```

If you're paying attention to Xcode, you'll notice that the method availableSymbols() is grayed out in the code's autocompletion:

You'll also see the compiler rightfully complain:

```
Invalid conversion from 'async' function of type '() async
throws -> Void' to synchronous function type '() -> Void'
```

Xcode tells you that onAppear(...) runs code synchronously; however, you're trying to call an asynchronous function in that non-concurrent context.

Luckily, you can use the `.task(priority:_:)` view modifier instead of `onAppear(...)`, which will allow you to call asynchronous functions right away.

Remove `onAppear(...)` and replace it with:

```
.task {
  guard symbols.isEmpty else { return }
}
```

`task(priority:_:)` allows you to call asynchronous functions and, similarly to `onAppear(_:)`, is called when the view appears onscreen. That's why you start by making sure you don't have symbols already.

Now, to call your new async function, append the following inside the `task { ... }` modifier:

```
do {
  symbols = try await model.availableSymbols()
} catch {

}
```

As before, you use both `try` and `await` to signify that the method might either throw an error or asynchronously return a value. You assign the result to `symbols`, and ... that's all you need to do here.

You'll notice that the `catch` portion is still empty. You'll definitely want to handle the erroneous case where `availableSymbols` can't provide a valid response.

The UI in the starter project has already been wired to display an alert box if you update `lastErrorMessage`, so you'll use that functionality here. Add the following line inside the empty `catch` block:

```
lastErrorMessage = error.localizedDescription
```

Swift catches the error, regardless of which thread throws it. You simply write your error handling code as if your code is entirely synchronous. Amazing!

Quickly check that the server is still running in your Terminal, then build and run the app.

As soon as the app launches, you'll briefly see an activity indicator and then a list of stock symbols:

Awesome! Your next task is to test that the asynchronous error handling works as expected. Switch to Terminal and press **Control-C** to stop the book server.

Run your project one more time. Now, your catch block will handle the error and assign it to lastErrorMessage. Then, the SwiftUI code will pick it up and an alert box will pop up:

Writing modern Swift code isn't that difficult after all, is it?

I get it if you're excited about how few lines you needed here for your networking. To be honest, I'm excited, too; I really needed to restrain myself from ending every sentence with an exclamation mark!

Using Asynchronous Sequences

Even though this chapter is just an introduction, you'll also get to try out some more advanced topics — namely, asynchronous sequences.

Asynchronous sequences are similar to the "vanilla" Swift sequences from the standard library. The *hook* of asynchronous sequences is that you can iterate over their elements asynchronously as more and more elements become available over time.

Open **TickerView.swift**. This is a SwiftUI view, similar in structure to SymbolListView. It revolves around a ForEach that displays stock price changes over time.

In the previous section, you "fired" an async network request, waited for the result, and then returned it. For TickerView, that same approach won't work because you can't wait for the request to complete and *only then* display the data. The data needs to keep coming in indefinitely and bring in those price updates.

Here, the server will send you a single long-living response, adding more and more text to it over time. Each text line is a complete JSON array that you can decode on its own:

```
[{"AAPL": 102.86}, {"BABA": 23.43}]
// .. waits a bit ...
[{"AAPL": 103.45}, {"BABA": 23.08}]
// .. waits some more ...
[{"AAPL": 103.67}, {"BABA": 22.10}]
// .. waits even some more ...
[{"AAPL": 104.01}, {"BABA": 22.17}]
// ... continuous indefinitely ...
```

On the live ticker screen, you'll iterate over each line of the response and update the prices onscreen in real time!

In TickerView, find .padding(.horizontal). Directly below that line, add a task modifier and call the model's method that starts the live price updates:

```
.task {
  do {
    try await model.startTicker(selectedSymbols)
  } catch {
    lastErrorMessage = error.localizedDescription
  }
}
```

The code looks similar to what you did in SymbolListView, except that the method doesn't return a result. You'll be handling continuous updates, not a single return value.

Open **LittleJohnModel.swift** and find the startTicker(_:) placeholder method, where you'll add your live updates. A published property called tickerSymbols is already wired up to the UI in the ticker screen, so updating this property will propagate the changes to your view.

Next, add the following code to the end of startTicker(_:):

```
let (stream, response) = try await liveURLSession.bytes(from:
url)
```

URLSession.bytes(from:delegate:) is similar to the API you used in the previous section. However, instead of data, it returns an asynchronous sequence that you can iterate over time. It's assigned to stream in your code.

Additionally, instead of using the shared URL session, you use a custom pre-configured session called liveURLSession, which makes requests that never expire or time out. This lets you keep receiving a super-long server response indefinitely.

Just as before, the first thing to do is check for a successful response code. Add the following code at the end of the same function:

```
guard (response as? HTTPURLResponse)?.statusCode == 200 else {
  throw "The server responded with an error."
}
```

Now comes the fun part. Append a new loop:

```
for try await line in stream.lines {

}
```

stream is a sequence of bytes that the server sends as a response. lines is an abstraction of that sequence that gives you that response's lines of text, one by one. You'll iterate over the lines and decode each one as JSON.

To do that, insert the following inside the `for` loop:

```
let sortedSymbols = try JSONDecoder()
  .decode([Stock].self, from: Data(line.utf8))
  .sorted(by: { $0.name < $1.name })

tickerSymbols = sortedSymbols
print("Updated: \(Date())")
```

If the decoder successfully decodes the line as a list of symbols, you sort them and assign them to `tickerSymbols` to render them onscreen. If the decoding fails, `JSONDecoder` simply throws an error.

Run the book server again if it's still turned off from your last error handling test. Then, build and run the app. In the first screen, select a few stocks:

Then tap **Live ticker** to see the live price updates on the next screen:

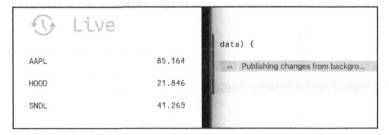

Though you'll most likely see some price updates, you'll also notice glitches and a big purple warning in your code editor saying `Publishing changes from background threads is not allowed`....

Updating Your UI From the Main Thread

Earlier, you published updates by updating a @State property, and SwiftUI took care to route the updates through the main thread. Now, you update tickerSymbols from within the same context where you're running your asynchronous work, without specifying that it's a UI update, so the code ends up running on an arbitrary thread in the pool.

This causes SwiftUI some grief because it naturally expects your code to be kosher when it updates the UI.

Luckily, you can switch to the main thread any time you need to. MainActor is a type that runs code on the main thread. You can easily run any code with it by calling MainActor.run(_:).

However, for model classes that drive your UI, you might as well assign all your model code to run on the main actor. Scroll up in the file and annotate LittleJohnModel with @MainActor, like so:

```
@MainActor class LittleJohnModel: ObservableObject {
```

Run the app and go to the live prices screen. This time around, you'll see the prices continuously go up and down:

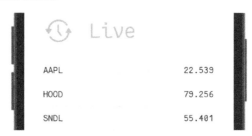

Hopefully, you enjoyed this first encounter with asynchronous sequences. You'll learn a great deal more about them in Chapter 3, "AsyncSequence & Intermediate Task".

Canceling Tasks in Structured Concurrency

As mentioned earlier, one of the big leaps for concurrent programming with Swift is that modern, concurrent code executes in a structured way. Tasks run in a strict hierarchy, so the runtime knows who's the parent of a task and which features new tasks should inherit.

For example, look at the task(_:) modifier in TickerView. Your code calls startTicker(_:) asynchronously. In turn, startTicker(_:) asynchronously *awaits* URLSession.bytes(from:delegate:), which returns an async sequence that you iterate over:

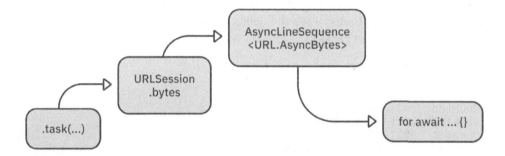

At each suspension point — that is, every time you see the await keyword — the thread could potentially change. Since you start the entire process inside task(_:), the async task is the parent of all those other tasks, regardless of their execution thread or suspension state.

The task(_:) view modifier in SwiftUI takes care of canceling your asynchronous code when its view goes away.

Thanks to structured concurrency, which you'll learn much more about later in this book, all asynchronous tasks are also canceled when the user navigates out of the screen.

To verify how this works in practice, navigate to the updates screen and look at the Xcode console to check that you see the debug prints from `LittleJohnModel.startTicker(_:)`:

```
Updated: 2021-08-12 18:24:12 +0000
Updated: 2021-08-12 18:24:13 +0000
Updated: 2021-08-12 18:24:14 +0000
Updated: 2021-08-12 18:24:15 +0000
Updated: 2021-08-12 18:24:16 +0000
Updated: 2021-08-12 18:24:17 +0000
Updated: 2021-08-12 18:24:18 +0000
```

Now, tap **Back**. `TickerView` disappears and the `task(_:)` view modifier's task is canceled. This cancels all child tasks, including the call to `LittleJohnModel.startTicker(_:)`. As a result, the debug logs in the console stop as well, verifying that all execution ends!

Now, you've finished working on LittleJohn. Congratulations, you completed the first project in this book!

Stick around if you'd like to work through a challenge on your own. Otherwise, turn the page and move on to learning about `async/await` and `Task` in more detail!

Challenges

Challenge: Adding Extra Error Handling

There's one edge case that the app still doesn't handle graciously: What if the server becomes unavailable while the user is observing the price updates?

You can reproduce this situation by navigating to the prices screen, then stopping the server by pressing **Control-C** in the terminal window.

No error messages pop up in the app because there is no error, per se. In fact, the response sequence simply completes when the server closes it. In this case, your code continues to execute with no error, but it produces no more updates.

In this challenge, you'll add code to reset LittleJohnModel.tickerSymbols when the async sequence ends and then navigate out of the updates screen.

In LittleJohnModel.startTicker(_:), after the for loop, append code to set tickerSymbols to an empty array if the async sequence unexpectedly ends.

Next, in TickerView, add a new view modifier that observes the number of observed ticker symbols and dismisses the view if the selection resets:

```
.onChange(of: model.tickerSymbols.count) { newValue in
  if newValue == 0 {
    presentationMode.wrappedValue.dismiss()
  }
}
```

Note that the starter already includes an environment presentationMode ready to use.

If everything goes well, when you stop the server while watching the live updates in the app, LittleJohn will automatically dismiss the updates screen and go back to the list of symbols.

If you get stuck in the challenge or if something doesn't work as you expect, be sure to check the solution in this chapter's materials.

Key Points

- Swift 5.5 introduced a **new concurrency model** that solves many of the existing concurrency issues, like thread explosion, priority inversion, and loose integration with the language and the runtime.

- The `async` keyword defines a function as asynchronous. `await` lets you wait in a non-blocking fashion for the result of the asynchronous function.

- Use the `task(priority:_:)` view modifier as an `onAppear(_:)` alternative when you want to run asynchronous code.

- You can naturally loop over an asynchronous sequence over time by using a `for try await` loop syntax.

Chapter 2: Getting Started With async/await

By Marin Todorov

Now that you know what Swift Concurrency is and why you should use it, you'll spend this chapter diving deeper into the async/await syntax and how it coordinates asynchronous execution.

You'll also learn about the Task type and how to use it to create new asynchronous execution contexts.

Before that, though, you'll spend a moment learning about pre-Swift 5.5 concurrency as opposed to the new async/await syntax.

Pre-async/await Asynchrony

Up until Swift 5.5, writing asynchronous code had many shortcomings. Take a look at the following example:

```
func fetchStatus(completion: @escaping (ServerStatus) -> Void) {
  URLSession.shared.dataTask(
    with: URL(string: "http://amazingserver.com/status")!
  ) { data, response, error in
    // Decoding, error handling, etc
    completion(ServerStatus(data))
  }
  .resume()
}

fetchStatus { [weak viewModel] status in
  guard let viewModel else { return }
  viewModel.serverStatus = status
}
```

This is a short block of code that performs a network request and assigns its result to a property of your view model. It's deceptively simple, yet it creates *a lot* of room for coding errors!

Take a moment to inspect the code above. You might notice that:

- The compiler has no clear way of knowing how many times you'll call `completion` inside `fetchServerStatus()`. Therefore, it can't optimize its lifespan and memory usage.

- You need to handle memory management yourself by weakly capturing `viewModel`, then checking in the code to see if it was released before the closure runs.

- The compiler has no way to make sure you handled the error. In fact, if you forget to handle `error` in the closure, or don't invoke `completion` altogether, the method will silently freeze.

- And the list goes on and on...

The modern concurrency model in Swift works closely with both the compiler *and* the runtime. It provides the following three tools to achieve the same goals as the example above:

- **async**: Indicates that a method or function is asynchronous. Using it lets you *suspend* execution until an asynchronous method returns a result.

- **await**: Indicates that your code might pause its execution while it waits for an `async`-annotated method or function to return.

- **Task**: A unit of asynchronous work. You can wait for a task to complete or cancel it before it finishes.

Here's what you get when you rewrite the code from earlier using modern concurrency syntax:

```
func fetchStatus() async throws -> ServerStatus {
    let (data, _) = try await URLSession.shared.data(
      from: URL(string: "http://amazingserver.com/status")!
    )
    return ServerStatus(data: data)
}

Task {
    viewModel.serverStatus = try await api.fetchStatus()
}
```

The code above has about the same number of lines as the earlier example, but the intent is clearer to both the compiler and the runtime. Specifically:

- **fetchStatus()** is an asynchronous function that can suspend and resume execution. You mark it with the `async` keyword.

- **fetchStatus()** either returns `Data` or throws an error. This is checked at compile time — no more worrying about forgetting to handle an erroneous code path!

- **Task** executes the given closure in an asynchronous context so the compiler can protect you from writing unsafe code in that closure.

- Finally, you give the runtime an opportunity to suspend or cancel your code every time you call an asynchronous function by using the **await** keyword. This lets the system constantly change the priorities in the current task queue.

Separating Code Into Partial Tasks

Above, you saw that "the code might suspend at each `await`" — but what does that mean? To optimize shared resources such as CPU cores and memory, Swift *splits up* your code into logical units called **partial tasks**, or **partials**. These represent parts of the code you'd like to run asynchronously.

```
func myFunction () async throws {
  let log =      try await serverLog ( )

  for   try await line in log.lines   {

    if   try await line.isConnected   {

      await sendLogLine (line)

    }
  }
}
```

The Swift runtime schedules each of these pieces separately for asynchronous execution. When each partial task completes, the system decides whether to continue with your code or to execute another task.

That's why it's important to remember that each of these `await`-annotated partial tasks might run on a different thread at the system's discretion. You shouldn't make assumptions about the app's state after an `await`; although two lines of code appear one after another, they often execute some time apart.

To recap, `async/await` is a simple syntax that packs a lot of punch. It lets the compiler guide you in writing safe and solid code, while the runtime optimizes for a well-coordinated use of shared system resources.

Executing Partial Tasks

As opposed to the closure syntax mentioned at the beginning of this chapter, the modern concurrency syntax is light on ceremony. The keywords you use, such as `async`, `await` and `let`, clearly express your intent.

The foundation of the concurrency model revolves around breaking asynchronous code into partial tasks that you execute on an **Executor**.

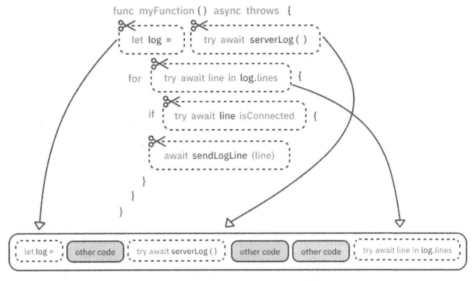

Executor

Note: In the current version of Swift, the built-in executor runs tasks as an asynchronous sequence only. There is already, however, a proposal and a work-in-progress implementation for custom executors that would unlock much more flexible task scheduling.

Controlling a Task's Lifetime

One essential new feature of modern concurrency is the system's ability to manage the lifetime of the asynchronous code.

A big shortcoming of older multi-threaded APIs was that, once an asynchronous piece of code started executing, it was very difficult to meaningfully cancel that work.

A good example of this is a service that fetches content from a remote server. If you call this service twice, the system doesn't have any automatic mechanism to reclaim resources that the first, now-unneeded call used, which is an unnecessary waste of resources.

The new model breaks your code into partials, providing suspension points where you check in with the runtime. This gives the system the opportunity to not only suspend your code but to **cancel it** altogether, at its discretion.

Thanks to the new asynchronous model, when you cancel a given task, the runtime can walk down the async hierarchy and cancel all the child tasks as well.

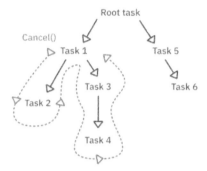

But what if you have a hard-working task performing long, tedious computations without any suspension points? For such cases, Swift provides APIs to detect if the current task has been canceled. If so, you can manually give up its execution.

Finally, the suspension points also offer an **escape route** for errors to bubble up the hierarchy to the code that catches and handles them.

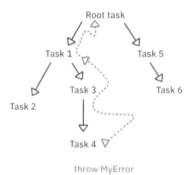

The new model provides an error-handling infrastructure similar to the one that synchronous functions have, using modern and well-known **throwing functions**. It also optimizes for quick memory release as soon as a task throws an error.

You already see that the recurring topics in the modern Swift concurrency model are safety, optimized resource usage and minimal syntax. Throughout the rest of this chapter, you'll learn about these new APIs in detail and try them out for yourself.

Getting Started

SuperStorage is an app that lets you browse files you've stored in the cloud and download them for local, on-device preview. It offers three different "subscription plans", each with its own download options: "Silver", "Gold" and "Cloud 9".

Open the starter version of SuperStorage in this chapter's materials, under **projects/ starter**. Like all projects in this book, **SuperStorage**'s SwiftUI views, navigation and data model are already wired up and ready to go. This app has more UI code compared to **LittleJohn**, which you worked on in the previous chapter, but it provides more opportunities to get your hand dirty with some asynchronous work.

> **Note**: The server returns mock data for you to work with; it is not, in fact, a working cloud solution. It also lets you reproduce slow downloads and erroneous scenarios, so don't mind the download speed. There's nothing wrong with your machine.

While working on SuperStorage in this and the next chapter, you'll create async functions, design some concurrent code, use async sequences and more.

A Bird's Eye View of async/await

async/await has a few different flavors depending on what you intend to do:

- To declare a function as asynchronous, add the async keyword before throws or the return type. Call the function by prepending await and, if the function is throwing, try as well. Here's an example:

```
func myFunction() async throws -> String {
  ...
}

let myVar = try await myFunction()
```

- To make a computed property asynchronous, simply add async to the getter and access the value by prepending await, like so:

```
var myProperty: String {
  get async {
    ...
  }
}

print(await myProperty)
```

- For closures, add async to the signature:

```
func myFunction(worker: (Int) async -> Int) -> Int {
  ...
}

myFunction {
  return await computeNumbers($0)
}
```

Now that you've had a quick overview of the async/await syntax, it's time to try it for yourself.

Getting the List of Files From the Server

Your first task is to add a method to the app's model that fetches a list of available files from the web server in JSON format. This task is almost identical to what you did in the previous chapter, but you'll cover the code in more detail.

Open **SuperStorageModel.swift** and add a new method anywhere inside
SuperStorageModel:

```
func availableFiles() async throws -> [DownloadFile] {
  guard let url = URL(string: "http://localhost:8080/files/
list") else {
    throw "Could not create the URL."
  }
}
```

Don't worry about the compiler error Xcode shows; you'll finish this method's body
momentarily.

You annotate the method with async throws to make it a **throwing, asynchronous
function**. This tells the compiler and the Swift runtime how you plan to use it:

- The compiler makes sure you don't call this function from synchronous contexts
  where the function can't suspend and resume the task.

- The runtime uses the new cooperative thread pool to schedule and execute the
  method's partial tasks.

In the method, you fetch a list of decodable DownloadFiles from a given url. Each
DownloadedFile represents one file available in the user's cloud.

Making the Server Request

At the end of the method's body, add this code to execute the server request:

```
let (data, response) = try await
  URLSession.shared.data(from: url)
```

You use the shared URLSession to asynchronously fetch the data from the given
URL. It's vital that you do this asynchronously because doing so lets the system use
the thread to do other work while it waits for a response. It doesn't block others from
using the shared system resources.

Each time you see the await keyword, think **suspension point**. The current code
will suspend execution, the code you await will execute or let other higher-priority
work run before it and finally, if your code throws, that error will bubble up the call
hierarchy to the nearest catch statement.

Each await funnels the execution through a system, which prioritizes jobs,
propagates cancellation, bubbles up errors, and more.

Verifying the Response Status

Once the asynchronous call completes successfully and returns the server response data, you can verify the response status and decode the data as usual.

Add the following code at the end of `availableFiles()`:

```
guard (response as? HTTPURLResponse)?.statusCode == 200 else {
  throw "The server responded with an error."
}

guard let list = try? JSONDecoder()
  .decode([DownloadFile].self, from: data) else {
  throw "The server response was not recognized."
}
```

You first inspect the response's HTTP status code to confirm it's indeed **HTTP 200 OK**. Then, you use a `JSONDecoder` to decode the raw response to an array of `DownloadFiles`.

Returning the List of Files

Once you decode the JSON into a list of `DownloadFile` values, you need to return it as the asynchronous result of your function. How simple is it to do that? Very.

Simply add the following line to the end of `availableFiles()`:

```
return list
```

While the execution of the method is entirely *asynchronous*, the code reads entirely *synchronously* which makes it relatively easy to maintain, understand and reason about.

Displaying the List

You can now use this new method to feed the file list on the app's main screen. Open **ListView.swift** and add one more view modifier directly after `.alert(...)`, near the bottom of the file:

```
.task {
  guard files.isEmpty else { return }

  do {
    files = try await model.availableFiles()
  } catch {
```

```
        lastErrorMessage = error.localizedDescription
      }
   }
```

As mentioned in the previous chapter, `task` is a view modifier that allows you to execute asynchronous code when the view appears. It also handles canceling the asynchronous execution when the view disappears.

In the code above, you:

1. Check if you already fetched the file list; if not, you call `availableFiles()` to do that.

2. Catch and store any errors in `lastErrorMessage`. The app will then display the error message in an alert box.

Testing the Error Handling

If the book server is still running from the previous chapter, stop it. Then, build and run the project. Your code inside `.task(...)` will catch a networking error, like so:

Asynchronous functions propagate errors up the call hierarchy, just like synchronous Swift code. If you ever wrote Swift code with asynchronous error handling before `async/await`'s arrival, you're undoubtedly ecstatic about the new way to handle errors.

Viewing the File List

Now, start the book server. If you haven't already done that, navigate to the server folder **00-book-server** in the book materials-repository and enter `swift run`. The detailed steps are covered in Chapter 1, "Why Modern Swift Concurrency?".

Restart the SuperStorage app and you'll see a list of files:

Notice there are a few TIFF and JPEG images in the list. These two image formats will give you various file sizes to play with from within the app.

Getting the Server Status

Next, you'll add one more asynchronous function to the app's model to fetch the server's status and get the user's usage quota.

Open **SuperStorageModel.swift** and add the following method to the class:

```
func status() async throws -> String {
  guard let url = URL(string: "http://localhost:8080/files/
status") else {
    throw "Could not create the URL."
  }
}
```

A successful server response returns the status as a text message, so your new function asynchronously returns a `String` as well.

As you did before, add the code to asynchronously get the response data and verify the status code:

```
let (data, response) = try await
  URLSession.shared.data(from: url, delegate: nil)

guard (response as? HTTPURLResponse)?.statusCode == 200 else {
  throw "The server responded with an error."
}
```

Finally, decode the response and return the result:

```
return String(decoding: data, as: UTF8.self)
```

The new method is now complete and follows the same pattern as
availableFiles().

Showing the Service Status

For your next task, you'll use status() to show the server status in the file list.

Open **ListView.swift** and add this code inside the .task(...) view modifier, after
assigning files:

```
status = try await model.status()
```

Build and run. You'll see some server usage data at the bottom of the file list:

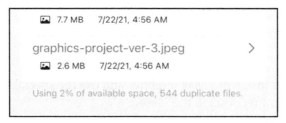

Everything works great so far, but there's a hidden optimization opportunity you
might have missed. Can you guess what it is? Move on to the next section for the
answer.

Grouping Asynchronous Calls

Revisit the code currently inside the task modifier:

```
files = try await model.availableFiles()
status = try await model.status()
```

Both calls are asynchronous and, in theory, could happen at the same time. However,
by explicitly marking them with await, the call to status() doesn't start until the
call to availableFiles() completes.

Sometimes, you need to perform sequential asynchronous calls — like when you want to use data from the first call as a parameter of the second call.

```
let result1 = await serverCall1()

let result2 = await serverCall2(result1)

let result3 = await serverCall3(result2)
```

This isn't the case here, though!

For all you care, both server calls can be made *at the same time* because they don't depend on each other. But how can you await *both* calls without them blocking each other? Swift solves this problem with a feature called **structured concurrency**, via the async let syntax.

Using async let

Swift offers a special syntax that lets you group several asynchronous calls and await them all together.

Remove all the code inside the task modifier and use the special async let syntax to run two concurrent requests to the server:

```
guard files.isEmpty else { return }

do {
  async let files = try model.availableFiles()
  async let status = try model.status()
} catch {
  lastErrorMessage = error.localizedDescription
}
```

An async let binding allows you to create a local constant that's similar to the concept of promises in other languages. **Option-Click** files to bring up Quick Help:

> **Summary**
> No overview available.
>
> **Declaration**
>
> `async let files: [DownloadFile]`
>
> **Declared In**
> ListView.swift
>
> 104   do {

The declaration explicitly includes `async let`, which means you can't access the value without an `await`.

The `files` and `status` bindings promise that either the values of the specific types or an error will be available later.

To read the binding results, you need to use `await`. If the value is already available, you'll get it immediately. Otherwise, your code will suspend at the `await` until the result becomes available:

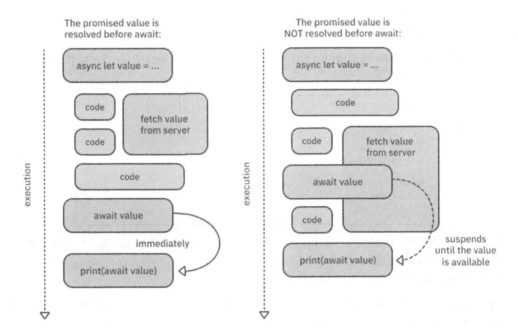

> **Note**: An `async let` binding feels similar to a promise in other languages, but in Swift, the syntax integrates much more tightly with the runtime. It's not just syntactic sugar but a feature implemented into the language.

Extracting Values From the Two Requests

Looking at the last piece of code you added, there's a *small detail* you need to pay attention to: The async code in the two calls starts executing right away, *before* you call `await`. So `status` and `availableFiles` run in parallel to your main code, inside the `task` modifier.

To group concurrent bindings and extract their values, you have two options:

- Group them in a collection, such as an array.

- Wrap them in parentheses as a tuple and then destructure the result.

The two syntaxes are interchangeable. Since you have only two bindings, you'll use the tuple syntax here.

Insert this code at the end of the do block:

```
let (filesResult, statusResult) = try await (files, status)
```

And what are `filesResult` and `statusResult`? **Option-Click** `filesResults` to check for yourself:

Summary
No overview available.

Declaration

```
let filesResult: [DownloadFile]
```

Declared In
ListView.swift

```
    106                    async let status = try model.status()
```

This time, the declaration is simply a `let` constant, which indicates that by the time you can access `filesResult` and `statusResult`, both requests have finished their work and provided you with a final result.

At this point in the code, if an `await` didn't throw in the meantime, you know that all the concurrent bindings resolved successfully.

Updating the View

Now that you have both the file list and the server status, you can update the view. Insert the following two lines at the end of the do block:

```
self.files = filesResult
self.status = statusResult
```

Build and run. This time, you execute the server requests in parallel, and the UI becomes ready for the user a little faster than before.

Take a moment to appreciate that the same `async`, `await` and `let` syntax lets you run non-blocking asynchronous code serially and *also* in parallel. That's some amazing API design right there!

Asynchronously Downloading a File

Open **SuperStorageModel.swift** and scroll to the method called `download(file:)`. The starter code in this method creates the endpoint URL for downloading files. It returns empty data to make the starter project compile successfully.

`SuperStorageModel` includes two methods to manage the current app downloads:

- **addDownload(name:)**: Adds a new file to the list of ongoing downloads.

- **updateDownload(name:progress:)**: Updates the given file's progress.

You'll use these two methods to update the model and the UI.

Downloading the Data

To perform the actual download, add the following code directly before the `return` line in `download(file:)`:

```
addDownload(name: file.name)

let (data, response) = try await
  URLSession.shared.data(from: url, delegate: nil)

updateDownload(name: file.name, progress: 1.0)
```

`addDownload(name:)` adds the file to the published `downloads` property of the model class. `DownloadView` uses it to display the ongoing download statuses onscreen.

Then, you fetch the file from the server. Finally, you update the progress to `1.0` to indicate the download finished.

Adding Server Error Handling

To handle any possible server errors, also append the following code before the `return` statement:

```
guard (response as? HTTPURLResponse)?.statusCode == 200 else {
  throw "The server responded with an error."
}
```

Finally, replace `return Data()` with:

```
return data
```

Admittedly, emitting progress updates here is not very useful because you jump from 0% directly to 100%. However, you'll improve this in the next chapter for the premium subscription plans — Gold and Cloud 9.

For now, open **DownloadView.swift**. Scroll to the code that instantiates the file details view, `FileDetails(...)`, then find the closure parameter called `downloadSingleAction`.

This is the action for the leftmost button — the cheapest download plan in the app.

So far, you've only used `.task()` in SwiftUI code to run async calls. But how would you await `download(file:)` inside the `downloadSingleAction` closure, which doesn't accept async code?

Add this inside the closure to double-check that the closure expects synchronous code:

```
fileData = try await model.download(file: file)
```

The error states that your code is asynchronous — it's of type `() async throws -> Void` — but the parameter expects a synchronous closure of type `() -> Void`.

One viable solution is to change `FileDetails` to accept an asynchronous closure. But what if you don't have access to the source code of the API you want to use? Fortunately, there is another way.

Running async Requests From a non-async Context

While still in **DownloadView.swift**, replace `fileData = try await model.download(file: file)` with:

```
Task {
  fileData = try await model.download(file: file)
}
```

As your learned in the previous chapter, you'll usually use `Task` to code in an asynchronous context. This feels like the perfect time to dive deeper into this type!

A Quick Detour Through Task

`Task` is a type that represents a **top-level asynchronous task**. Being top-level means it can *create* an asynchronous context — which can start from a synchronous context.

Long story short, any time you want to run asynchronous code from a synchronous context, you need a new `Task`.

You can use the following APIs to manually control a task's execution:

- **Task(priority:operation)**: Schedules `operation` for asynchronous execution with the given priority. It inherits defaults from the current synchronous context.

- **Task.detached(priority:operation)**: Similar to `Task(priority:operation)`, except that it doesn't inherit the defaults of the calling context.

- **Task.value**: Waits for the task to complete, then returns its value, similarly to a promise in other languages.

- **Task.isCancelled**: Returns `true` if the task was canceled since the last suspension point. You can inspect this boolean to know when you should stop the execution of scheduled work.

- **Task.checkCancellation()**: Throws a `CancellationError` if the task is canceled. This lets the function use the error-handling infrastructure to yield execution.

- **Task.sleep(for:)**: Makes the task suspend for at least the given duration and doesn't block the thread while that happens.

In the previous section, you used `Task(priority:operation:)`, which created a new asynchronous task with the `operation` closure and the given `priority`. By default, the task inherits its priority from the current context — so you can usually omit it.

You need to specify a priority, for example, when you'd like to create a low-priority task from a high-priority context or vice versa.

Don't worry if this seems like a lot of options. You'll try out many of these throughout the book, but for now, let's get back to the SuperStorage app.

> **Note**: It's worth reiterating the fact that `Task` creates **only** top-level tasks. If you nest syntactically two or more tasks (in other words they are nested visually in your code) that doesn't create a task hierarchy at runtime, they will all be top-level tasks.

Creating a New Task on a Different Actor

In the scenario above, `Task` runs on the actor that called it. To create the same task without it being a part of the actor, use `Task.detached(priority:operation:)`.

> **Note**: Don't worry if you don't know what actors are yet. This chapter mentions them briefly because they're a core concept of modern concurrency in Swift. You'll dig deeper into actors later in this book.

For now, remember that when your code creates a `Task` from the main thread, that task will run on the main thread, too. Therefore, you know you can update the app's UI safely.

Build and run one more time. Select one of the JPEG files and tap the **Silver plan** download button. You'll see a progress bar and, ultimately, a preview of the image.

However, you'll likely notice UI glitches, such as the progress bar only filling up halfway sometimes. That's a hint that you're updating the UI from a background thread.

And just as in the previous chapter, there's a log message in Xcode's console and a friendly purple warning in the code editor:

```
class SuperStorageModel: ObservableObject {
    /// The list of currently running downloads.
    @Published var downloads = [DownloadInfo]()   ⚠ Publishing changes from background
}
```

But why? You create your new async `Task` from your UI code on the main thread — and now *this* happens!

Remember, you learned that every use of `await` is a suspension point, and your code might resume on a different thread. The first piece of your code runs on the main thread because the task initially runs on the main actor. But after the first `await`, your code could be running on *any* thread.

You need to **explicitly** route any UI-driving code back to the main actor.

Routing Code to the Main Thread

One way to ensure your code is on the main thread is calling `MainActor.run()`, as you did in the previous chapter. The call looks something like this (no need to add this to your code):

```
await MainActor.run {
  ... your UI code ...
}
```

`MainActor` is a type that runs code on the main thread. It's the modern alternative to the well-known `DispatchQueue.main`, which you might have used in the past.

While it gets the job done, using `MainActor.run()` too often results in code with many closures, making it hard to read. A more elegant solution is to annotate specific methods, closures, or even functions — with `@MainActor`. This will route the annotated scope's work to the main actor transparently.

Using @MainActor

In this chapter, you'll annotate the two methods that update `downloads` to make sure those changes happen on the main UI thread.

Open **SuperStorageModel.swift** and prepend @MainActor to the definition of `addDownload(file:)`:

```
@MainActor func addDownload(name: String)
```

Do the same for `updateDownload(name:progress:)`:

```
@MainActor func updateDownload(name: String, progress: Double)
```

Any calls to those two methods will automatically run on the main actor — and, therefore, on the main thread.

Running the Methods Asynchronously

Routing the two methods to a specific actor (the main actor or any other actor) requires that you call them asynchronously, which gives the runtime a chance to suspend and resume your call on the correct actor.

Scroll to download(file:) and fix the two compile errors.

Replace the synchronous call to addDownload(name: file.name) with:

```
await addDownload(name: file.name)
```

Then, prepend await when calling updateDownload:

```
await updateDownload(name: file.name, progress: 1.0)
```

That clears up the compile errors. Build and run. This time, the UI updates smoothly with no runtime warnings.

> **Note**: To save space on your machine, the server always returns the same image.

Updating the Download Screen's Progress

Before you wrap up this chapter, there's one loose end to take care of. If you navigate back to the file list and select a different file, the download screen keeps displaying the progress from your previous download.

You can fix this quickly by resetting the model in onDisappear(...). Open **DownloadView.swift** and add one more modifier to body, just below toolbar(...):

```
.onDisappear {
  fileData = nil
  model.reset()
}
```

In here, you reset the file data and invoke reset() on the model too, which clears the download list.

That's it, you can now preview multiple files one after the other, and the app keeps behaving.

Challenges

Challenge: Displaying a Progress View While Downloading

In DownloadView, there's a state property called isDownloadActive. When you set this property to true, the file details view displays an activity indicator next to the filename.

For this challenge, your goal is to show the activity indicator when the file download starts and hide it again when the download ends.

Be sure to also hide the indicator when the download throws an error. Check the **projects/challenges** folder for this chapter in the chapter materials to compare your solution with the suggested one.

Key Points

- Functions, computed properties and closures marked with **async** run in an asynchronous context. They can suspend and resume one or more times.

- **await** *yields* the execution to the central async handler, which decides which pending job to execute next.

- An **async let** binding promises to provide a value or an error later on. You access its result using `await`.

- **Task()** creates an asynchronous context for running on the current actor. It also lets you define the task's priority.

- Similar to `DispatchQueue.main`, **MainActor** is a type that executes blocks of code, functions or properties on the main thread.

This chapter gave you a deeper understanding of how you can create, run and wait for asynchronous tasks and results using the new Swift concurrency model and the async/await syntax.

You might've noticed that you only dealt with asynchronous pieces of work that yield a *single* result. In the next chapter, you'll learn about `AsyncSequence`, which can emit multiple results for an asynchronous piece of work. See you there!

Chapter 3: AsyncSequence & Intermediate Task

By Marin Todorov

Throughout this book, you'll use async sequences to make your life easier when it comes to asynchronous programming. Async sequences make consuming asynchronous results as simple as iterating over a Swift sequence.

You've already tried async sequences briefly in Chapter 1, "Why Modern Swift Concurrency?", but you'll take a more detailed deep dive into them now.

You'll do this while continuing to work on the **SuperStorage** app from the last chapter, so you don't need an introduction to the project; you can jump right in. When you've finished working through this chapter, you'll have given SuperStorage parallel download superpowers.

Getting to Know AsyncSequence

AsyncSequence is a protocol describing a sequence that can produce elements **asynchronously**.

Its surface API is identical to the Swift standard library's Sequence, with one difference: You need to await the next element, since it might not be immediately available, as it would in a regular Sequence

Here are some common tasks you'd use an asynchronous sequence for:

- Iterating over the sequence in a for loop, using await and, if the AsyncSequence is throwing, try. The code suspends **at each loop iteration** to get the next value:

```
for try await item in asyncSequence {
  // Next item from `asyncSequence`
}
```

- Using the asynchronous alternative of a standard library iterator with a while loop. This is similar to using a synchronous sequence: You need to make an iterator and repeatedly call next() using await until the sequence is over:

```
var iterator = asyncSequence.makeAsyncIterator()
while let item = try await iterator.next() {
  ...
}
```

- Using standard sequence methods like dropFirst(_:), prefix(_:) and filter(_:):

```
for await item in asyncSequence
  .dropFirst(5)
  .prefix(10)
  .filter { $0 > 10 }
  .map { "Item: \($0)" } {
    ...
  }
```

- Using special raw-byte sequence wrappers, such as reading file contents or fetching data from a server URL:

```
let bytes = URL(fileURLWithPath: "myFile.txt").resourceBytes

for await character in bytes.characters {
  ...
}

for await line in bytes.lines {
  ...
}
```

- Creating custom sequences by adopting `AsyncSequence` in your own types.

- Finally, you can create your very own custom async sequences by leveraging `AsyncStream`. You'll learn all about this option in the next chapter.

For an overview of all the Apple-provided types that are asynchronous sequences, visit `AsyncSequence`'s online documentation (https://apple.co/3AS4Tkw). You'll find the available types listed under **Conforming Types**.

Getting Started With AsyncSequence

So far, you've done good work on the **SuperStorage** app including building the main screen, which displays a list of files. When the user selects a file, they see its details with three download options, one for each of the cloud service's subscription plans:

In the previous chapter, you coded the **Silver** download option which fetches the complete file in one go.

You'll start this chapter by implementing the **Gold** download option, which provides progressive UI updates as the file downloads.

You'll achieve this by reading the file as an asynchronous sequence of bytes from the server. This lets you update the progress bar as you receive the file's contents.

Adding Your Asynchronous Sequence

Open the **SuperStorage** project and go to **SuperStorageModel.swift**, scrolling to `downloadWithProgress(fileName:name:size:offset:)`. It already contains code to create the correct server URL. It also calls `addDownload(name:)` to add the download onscreen.

Next, insert this code directly before `downloadWithProgress(fileName:name:size:offset:)`'s return line:

```
let result: (downloadStream: URLSession.AsyncBytes, response:
URLResponse)
```

> **Note**: Be mindful of the exact method signature — there's a similarly called method but with less arguments. You'll want to insert the code inside the method with four arguments.

Unlike before, when you used `URLSession.data(for:delegate:)` to return `Data`, you'll use an alternative API that returns `URLSession.AsyncBytes`. This sequence gives you the bytes it receives from the URL request, asynchronously.

The HTTP protocol lets a server define that it supports a capability called **partial requests**. If the server supports it, you can ask it to return a **byte range** of the response, instead of the entire response at once.

To make things a little more interesting, you'll support both standard and partial requests in the app.

Using partial response functionality lets you split the file into parts and download them in parallel. You'll need this functionality when implementing the **Cloud 9** download option later in this chapter.

Continue by adding the code below to make a partial file request:

```swift
if let offset = offset {
  let urlRequest = URLRequest(url: url, offset: offset, length:
size)
  result = try await
    URLSession.shared.bytes(for: urlRequest, delegate: nil)

  guard (result.response as? HTTPURLResponse)?.statusCode == 206
else {
    throw "The server responded with an error."
  }
}
```

If the code specifies an `offset`, you create a URL request and pass it to
`URLSession.bytes(for:delegate:)`, which returns a tuple of the response details
and an async sequence that enumerates the bytes of the file.

This time, you check if the response code is **206**, indicating a successful partial
response.

Next, append the following `else` block, which handles a regular, non-partial request,
to complete your `if` statement:

```
else {
  result = try await URLSession.shared.bytes(from: url,
delegate: nil)

  guard (result.response as? HTTPURLResponse)?.statusCode == 200
  else {
    throw "The server responded with an error."
  }
}
```

The code above is similar to what you did previously except that, this time, you're
checking for a 200 status and a successful server response.

Regardless of whether you make a partial or standard request, you end up with an
asynchronous byte sequence available in `result.downloadStream`.

Using ByteAccumulator

Now, it's time to start iterating over the response bytes. In this chapter, you'll
implement custom logic to iterate over the bytes. You'll use a type called
`ByteAccumulator`, which is included with the starter project, to fetch batches of
bytes from the sequence.

Why do you need to process the file in batches? Not only is it more fun, but a file can
contain millions or billions of bytes. You don't want to update the UI after getting
each byte because that'll completely overwhelm the system and potentially block the
main thread for the duration of the download.

`ByteAccumulator` will help you collect all of the file's contents and update the UI only periodically, after fetching each batch of bytes:

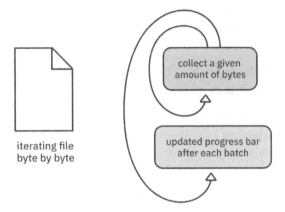

iterating file
byte by byte

collect a given
amount of bytes

updated progress bar
after each batch

> **Note**: If you're curious to see how the accumulator works, peek into **ByteAccumulator.swift**.

To start using `ByteAccumulator`, append this code before the return statement for `downloadWithProgress(fileName:name:size:offset:)` in `SuperStorageModel`:

```
var asyncDownloadIterator =
result.downloadStream.makeAsyncIterator()
```

AsyncSequence features a method called `makeAsyncIterator()`, which returns an asynchronous iterator for the sequence. You'll use the returned `asyncDownloadIterator` to iterate over the bytes, one at a time.

Now, to add the accumulator and collect all the bytes, add the code that creates and uses the accumulator:

```
var accumulator = ByteAccumulator(name: name, size: size)

while await !stopDownloads, !accumulator.checkCompleted() {

}
```

The first condition in the `while` loop checks if the model's `stopDownloads` flag isn't set. You'll use this flag again in a bit.

Please note that to read `stopDownloads`'s current value you need to use `await` — `stopDownloads` is isolated to the main actor so you must use await to access its value. You'll start learning about actors in Chapter 8, "Getting Started with Actors".

The second condition checks if `checkCompleted()` returns `false`, which means the accumulator can still collect more bytes.

The combination of these two conditions gives you the flexibility to run the loop until either the external flag `stopDownloads` is lifted or the accumulator completes the download. With this design, you're looking ahead and making the download code easily cancellable by using an external flag, if needed.

Next, insert the following code *inside* the `while` body:

```
while !accumulator.isBatchCompleted,
  let byte = try await asyncDownloadIterator.next() {
  accumulator.append(byte)
}
```

You use a second `while` loop that runs until the particular batch is full. The loop condition is similar to the outer `while` — you keep collecting bytes until either the `isBatchCompleted` flag is `true` or the byte sequence completes.

The code is so simple that if it weren't for the single `await` keyword in there, you couldn't tell it's asynchronously processing a file while downloading it at the same time.

Updating the Progress Bar

After a batch completes, the execution continues after the `while` loop. This is the perfect place to update the download progress bar. Insert the following code after the inner `while` loop, still inside the body of the outer `while` loop:

```
let progress = accumulator.progress
Task.detached(priority: .medium) {
  await self
    .updateDownload(name: name, progress: progress)
}

print(accumulator.description)
```

In the code above, you might spot at least a couple of novelties that you haven't covered yet.

First, you use `Task.detached(...)`. This is the *rogue* version of creating a task with `Task(priority:operation:)`. A detached task doesn't inherit the parent's priority, task storage or execution actor.

> **Note**: Generally speaking, the documentation recommends against using `Task.detached(...)` because it negatively affects the concurrency model's efficiency. In this case, you can use it in order to learn the syntax.

You create the task by explicitly setting a medium priority so there's no chance of it slowing down the ongoing download task. That task runs with `userInitiated` priority because it's a task started by a user action.

Another interesting aspect is that you capture `self` in the closure. Earlier, you learned that the new syntax mostly eliminates the need to manage memory manually. However, `SuperStorageModel` is a class — and, therefore, a reference type.

That means the usual memory management rules apply when you use escaping closures. It's not the case here, but if there's a chance you'll create a reference cycle, be sure to use `[weak self]` to capture a safe-to-use weak reference.

Last but not least, you calculate the current `progress`, hand it over to `updateDownload(...)` and you print the current accumulator state to the output console so you can keep track of downloads during development.

To make sure you inserted the code in the right places, you'll find the completed loop code below, so you can compare your code to it:

```
while await !stopDownloads, !accumulator.checkCompleted() {
  while !accumulator.isBatchCompleted,
    let byte = try await asyncDownloadIterator.next() {
    accumulator.append(byte)
  }
  let progress = accumulator.progress
  Task.detached(priority: .medium) {
    await self
      .updateDownload(name: name, progress: progress)
  }
  print(accumulator.description)
}
```

Returning the Accumulated Result

To wrap up the the method you worked on in the last sections, replace the line
`return Data()` with:

```
return accumulator.data
```

The newly completed method iterates over the download sequence and collects all
the bytes. It then updates the file progress at the end of each batch.

Switch to **DownloadView.swift** and scroll to the closure parameter called
`downloadWithUpdatesAction`. Insert this code inside the empty closure:

```
isDownloadActive = true
Task {
  do {
    fileData = try await model.downloadWithProgress(file: file)
  } catch { }
  isDownloadActive = false
}
```

The code above is identical to the code you added to `downloadSingleAction` in the
previous chapter. This time, however, it calls `downloadWithProgress(file:)` to
provide real-time updates to the progress bar.

This project interacts with the book-server web API. Before testing your code in the
iOS Simulator, make sure you're running the server app on your computer. To start
the server, navigate to the server folder in the book materials-repository and enter
`swift run`. The detailed steps are covered in more detail in Chapter 1, "Why Modern
Swift Concurrency?".

Build and run. Select a file and tap the **Gold** option to test your new code. You'll see
the progress bar update repeatedly as the file downloads:

Even more reassuring is the console output that the `while` loop prints after each batch:

```
[graphics-project-ver-1.jpeg] 0.9 MB
[graphics-project-ver-1.jpeg] 1 MB
[graphics-project-ver-1.jpeg] 1.2 MB
[graphics-project-ver-1.jpeg] 1.3 MB
[graphics-project-ver-1.jpeg] 1.4 MB
[graphics-project-ver-1.jpeg] 1.6 MB
...
```

This output tells you at what point in the download you're updating the progress bar, and you can easily calculate the size of each batch.

Congratulations, you now know most of what you need to know about using `AsyncSequence`!

Canceling Tasks

Canceling unneeded tasks is essential for the concurrency model to work efficiently.

When you use one of the new APIs, like `TaskGroup` (which you'll cover later in the book) or `async let`, the system can usually cancel the task automatically when needed.

You can, however, implement a finer-grained cancellation strategy for your task-based code by using the following `Task` APIs:

- **Task.isCancelled**: Returns `true` if the task is still alive but has been canceled since the last suspension point.

- **Task.currentPriority**: Returns the current task's priority.

- **Task.cancel()**: Attempts to cancel the task and its child tasks.

- **Task.checkCancellation()**: Throws a `CancellationError` if the task is canceled, making it easier to exit a throwing context.

- **Task.yield()**: Suspends the execution of the current task, giving the system a chance to cancel it automatically to execute some other task with higher priority.

When writing your asynchronous tasks, you'll choose which APIs to use depending on whether you need a throwing function like checkCancellation() or if you'd like to manage the control flow yourself by checking isCancelled.

In the next section, you'll implement your own custom logic to cancel download tasks that you don't need anymore.

Canceling an Asynchronous Task

To demonstrate why canceling tasks in a timely manner is important, run through the following scenario in the app:

Select one of the TIFF files and tap **Gold** to start a download with progress updates. Logs will appear in Xcode's console as the accumulator collects more and more of the file's content.

While the file is still downloading, tap the **< Back** button and observe the console. That download keeps going until it downloads the whole file!

Manually Canceling Tasks

So far, you wrote your async code inside a .task(...) view modifier, which is responsible for automatically canceling your code when the view disappears. But the actions for the download buttons *aren't* in a .task(), so there's nothing to cancel your async operations.

To fix this issue, you'll manually cancel your download tasks. Start by adding a new state property to DownloadView:

```
@State var downloadTask: Task<Void, Error>?
```

In downloadTask, you'll store an asynchronous task that returns no result and could throw an error. Task is a type like any other, so you can also store it in your view, model or any other scope. Task doesn't return anything if it's successful, so success is Void; likewise you return an Error if there's a failure.

Next, scroll back to downloadWithUpdatesAction and replace the line Task { with:

```
downloadTask = Task {
```

This stores the task in `downloadTask` so you can access it later. Most importantly, it lets you cancel the task at will.

You'll cancel the task when the user navigates back to the main screen. You already have some code in `.onDisappear(...)`. Add this line immediately after `model.reset()`:

```
downloadTask?.cancel()
```

Canceling `downloadTask` will also cancel all its child tasks — and all of their children, and so forth. Build and run the app. Then, try to run the test scenario from above. You'll notice that the progress logs in the console stop when you navigate back to the main screen.

Storing State in Tasks

Each asynchronous task executes in its own context, which consists of its priority, actor and more. But don't forget — a task can call other tasks. Because each might interact with many different functions, isolating shared data at runtime can be difficult.

To address this, Swift offers a new property wrapper that marks a given property as **task-local**. Think for a moment about injecting an object into the environment in SwiftUI, which makes the object available not only to the immediate `View`, but also to all of its child views.

Similarly, binding a task-local value makes it available not only to the immediate task, but also to all its child tasks:

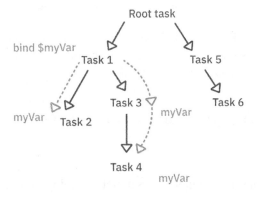

In this section of the chapter, you'll learn how to use task-local storage to make a function's behavior vary depending on the calling context.

More specifically, you'll code the action for the **Cancel All** button on the download screen.

Adding a Partial Image Preview

The JPEG format allows for partially decoding images, but other formats, such as TIFF, don't allow for partial preview. So you'll only support partial preview for JPEG files.

You'll develop the following custom logic: If the user is downloading a JPEG image and cancels before it finishes, you'll show the partially downloaded preview. For other image types, you'll just abort the download.

Open **SuperStorageModel.swift** and add a new property to `SuperStorageModel`:

```
@TaskLocal static var supportsPartialDownloads = false
```

If the user initiates a JPEG download, you'll set `supportsPartialDownloads` to `true`. You'll then add some new code in `SuperStorageModel` to provide the appropriate behavior based on the flag's value.

> **Note**: Task-local properties need to be either static for the type, or global variables.

The `@TaskLocal` property wrapper offers a method called `withValue()` that allows you to **bind a value** to an async task — or, simply speaking, **inject** it into a task hierarchy.

Open **DownloadView.swift**. In the downloadWithUpdatesAction closure parameter, replace the line fileData = try await model.downloadWithProgress(file: file) with these lines:

```
try await SuperStorageModel
  .$supportsPartialDownloads
  .withValue(file.name.hasSuffix(".jpeg")) {
    fileData = try await model.downloadWithProgress(file: file)
  }
```

Here, you use withValue(_:) to bind whether or not the download supports partial downloads, based on the file's extension. With the value bound, you call downloadWithProgress(file:).

You can bind multiple values this way, and you can also overwrite the values from inner bindings, like so (don't enter this code):

```
try await $property1.withValue(myData) {
  ...
  try await $property2.withValue(myConfig1) {
    ...
    try await serverRequest()
    try await $property2.withValue(myConfig2) {
      ...
    }
  }
}
```

In any case, you can see that using too many task-local storage properties might become difficult to read and reason about since you'll need to wrap the code in a closure for each binding.

> **Note**: In that sense, task storage is useful for binding fewer values: complete configuration objects or whole data models, rather than separate single values or flags as in the example above.

Adding the "Cancel All" Functionality

While still in **DownloadView.swift**, scroll down toward the bottom of the file and find .toolbar(...). This is where you define the **Cancel All** button. Its action closure is empty, so add the following code inside:

```
model.stopDownloads = true
```

This time, instead of canceling the download task altogether, like you did in .onDisappear(...), you turn on the stopDownloads flag on SuperStorageModel. You'll observe this flag while downloading. If it changes to true, you'll know that you need to cancel your tasks internally.

To do that, open **SuperStorageModel.swift** and scroll to downloadWithProgress(fileName:name:size:offset:). Toward the bottom of that function, insert this code just before the return line:

```
if await stopDownloads, !Self.supportsPartialDownloads {
  throw CancellationError()
}
```

This is the task-specific behavior for your custom cancellation. After each downloaded batch, you check if stopDownloads is true and, if so, also check whether the download supports partial preview.

Then:

- If Self.supportsPartialDownloads is false, you throw a CancellationError to exit the function with an error. This stops the download immediately.

- If Self.supportsPartialDownloads is true, you continue the execution and return the partially downloaded file content.

It's time to give that new feature a try. Build and run. Select a TIFF image, then start a **Gold** plan download. After a moment, tap **Cancel All**.

As you can see, the download stops. Your existing error-handling code catches the CancellationError and hides the spinner view without further updating the progress bar.

Now, try picking a JPEG image and running through the same routine:

Here, your *special* behavior for JPEG files returns the partially downloaded image, while DownloadView displays a preview of the successfully downloaded part.

Bridging Combine and AsyncSequence

Combine is Apple's reactive programming framework, based on the reactive streams specification. Its syntax is similar to RxSwift and other frameworks based on or inspired by the Rx standard. You can learn more about Combine by working through the book Combine: Asynchronous Programming With Swift (https://www.kodeco.com/books/combine-asynchronous-programming-with-swift).

Apple has integrated Combine into several key frameworks like Foundation and Core Data, among others:

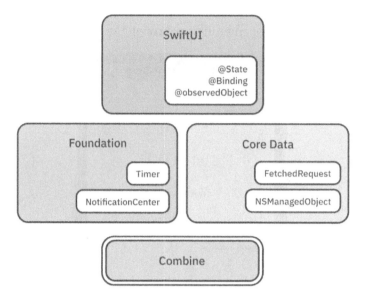

The simplicity of the `Publisher` protocol, which is the cornerstone of Combine, makes it universal and easy to adopt. A publisher can asynchronously emit zero, one or more values. It can, optionally, complete with a success or a failure:

values over time

Wait a minute!

That looks more or less precisely like an async sequence. Wouldn't it be fantastic if you could use `async/await` with all the existing Combine integrations from Apple, as well as with your own Combine code?

Yes, it would! And, fortunately, Apple offers an easy interface to do just that.

Adding a Progress Timer

In this section of the chapter, you'll add a timer showing how long the user's download is taking in real time:

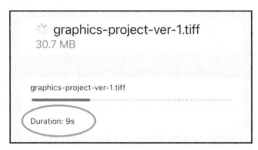

As usual, the starter project already includes the necessary UI code. DownloadView has a state property called `duration` that displays the duration below the progress bar.

The plan for the timer is to create a new async task whenever `isDownloadActive` changes to `true` and, in that task, create a Combine timer to update the UI periodically.

First, since you're using Combine, add one more import line at the top of **DownloadView.swift**:

```
import Combine
```

Then, add a new property in `DownloadedView` to store the timer task so you can cancel it when you're done:

```
@State var timerTask: Task<Void, Error>?
```

Next, find the property `@State var isDownloadActive = false`. The first thing you'd like to do when this flag is set to `true` or `false` is to cancel any previously running timer task. Add the following `didSet` accessor to `downloadTask`, so it looks like so:

```
@State var downloadTask: Task<Void, Error>? {
  didSet {
    timerTask?.cancel()
  }
}
```

Then, if the user just started a new download, you want to note the start time. Add this code next, still inside the `didSet` accessor:

```
guard isDownloadActive else { return }
let startTime = Date().timeIntervalSince1970
```

You'll use this later to calculate the duration based on the timer's start time.

Creating the Combine-based Timer

It's time to create the Combine timer and use the asynchronous `values` property to proxy your Combine code so you can use it with `await`.

Add this code to create a `Timer` publisher immediately after setting `startTime`:

```
let timerSequence = Timer
  .publish(every: 1, tolerance: 1, on: .main, in: .common)
  .autoconnect()
  .map { date -> String in
    let duration = Int(date.timeIntervalSince1970 - startTime)
    return "\(duration)s"
  }
  .values
```

Here's what this code is doing, step-by-step:

1. `Timer.publish` creates a Combine publisher that emits the current date every second.

2. `autoconnect` makes the publisher start ticking automatically whenever someone subscribes to it.

3. `map` calculates the elapsed time in seconds and returns the duration as a `String`.

4. Finally, and most importantly, `values` returns an *asynchronous sequence* of the publisher's events, which you can loop over as usual.

In fact, you can use `for await` with **any** Combine publisher by accessing its `values` property, which automatically wraps the publisher in an `AsyncSequence`.

> **Note**: Similarly, the `Future` type in Combine offers an async property called `value`. This lets you await the future result asynchronously.

Completing the Timer

Finally, still in the `didSet` accessor, add this code to create a new asynchronous task, store it in `timerTask` and loop over the sequence:

```
timerTask = Task {
  for await duration in timerSequence {
    self.duration = duration
  }
}
```

Here, you iterate over `timerSequence`. Inside that loop, you assign each value to `self.duration`. As mentioned in the beginning of the section, `duration` is already wired to the UI, so the only thing left to do is test it.

Build and run. Select a file and choose the **Gold** download button. You'll see that the duration summary appears below the progress bar and updates every second.

graphics-project-ver-1.tiff

Duration: 12s

Before wrapping up this chapter, there's one final easy-to-miss issue: Tap **Cancel All**, and you'll notice the timer is still running.

To fix this, scroll down to the `toolbar` modifier and add the following line to the `Button`'s `action` closure:

```
timerTask?.cancel()
```

This will cancel the pending timer whenever you tap the **Cancel All** button. That's it!

By completing the last task for this chapter, you've really become an async sequence pro user. If you're hungry for more practice, however, stay around and work through this chapter's challenge.

Challenges

Challenge: Implementing Concurrent Downloads for the "Cloud 9" Plan

To try creating local structured concurrency on your own, your challenge is to implement the **Cloud 9** download option. Don't worry, the starter project already comes with all the non-concurrency code, letting you focus on the essential bits and pieces.

First, head to **DownloadView.swift** and, inside the `downloadMultipleAction` closure parameter, add a call to `multiDownloadWithProgress(file:)` on your model. This is just like what you did for the other download buttons.

Once you do that, head to **SuperStorageModel.swift** and find `multiDownloadWithProgress(file:)`.

You'll see that the function already includes code to break the file download into four parts and store them in the `parts` array. Each array element has the following properties:

- **name**: The part name.

- **size**: The part size in bytes.

- **offset**: The part's offset within the complete file.

Luckily, these are also the exact parameters that `downloadWithProgress(fileName:name:size:offset)` expects, so putting the pieces together shouldn't be too difficult.

On your own, you should:

1. Define four promises with `async let` that each use `downloadWithProgress(fileName:name:size:offset)` to download a part of the file. Use the data in `parts`.

2. Await all four downloads together to execute them concurrently.

3. Combine the data from all the downloads to return the complete file content as the return value of `multiDownloadWithProgress(file:)`.

Once you've done all of the above, verify that tapping the **Cloud 9** button kicks off four simultaneous downloads, like so:

The most telling sign that everything works as expected will be that the image preview appears correctly at the end of the download:

If you get stuck or want to compare your solution with what I had in mind for this code, look at the completed challenge project in this chapter's materials.

Key Points

- `AsyncSequence` is a protocol which resembles `Sequence` and allows you to iterate over a sequence of values asynchronously.

- You iterate over a sequence asynchronously by using the `for await ... in` syntax, or directly creating an `AsyncIterator` and `awaiting` its `next()` method in the context of a `while` loop.

- `Task` offers several APIs to check if the current task was canceled. If you want to throw an error upon cancellation, use `Task.checkCancellation()`. To safely check and implement custom cancellation logic, use `Task.isCancelled`.

- To bind a value to a task and all its children, use the `@TaskLocal` property wrapper along with `withValue()`.

Earlier in this chapter, you learned there are a few ways to create your very own custom asynchronous sequence. Next, it seems like the perfect time to take a deep dive into `AsyncStream`, which lets you succinctly create your own asynchronous streams.

See you in the next chapter!

Chapter 4: Custom Asynchronous Sequences With AsyncStream

By Marin Todorov

In previous chapters, you've learned a few different ways to integrate asynchronous code in your apps. By now, you're hopefully comfortable calling and writing `async` functions and iterating over asynchronous sequences.

In this chapter, you'll dive deeper into how to create your very own custom async sequences using `AsyncStream`. Using this method grants you complete control over the asynchronous sequence and makes it trivial to wrap your own existing asynchronous APIs as async sequences.

In this chapter, you'll work through the **Blabber** app to explore these topics.

Getting Started With the Blabber App

Blabber is a messaging app that lets you chat with friends. It has some neat features like location sharing, a countdown timer and a friendly — but somewhat unpredictable — chatbot.

Like all projects in this book, Blabber's SwiftUI views, navigation and data model are already wired up and ready for you. Blabber has a similar foundation to the projects you've already worked on, like LittleJohn and SuperStorage. It's a connected app powered by a server API. Some of that code is already included in the starter because it works the same as in earlier projects.

Open the starter version of Blabber in this chapter's materials, under **projects/ starter**. When you complete the app, it will feature a working login screen, where you can choose your user name, and a chat screen to socialize with friends:

At the moment, you can enter a user name, but nothing else works. Your goal is to make asynchronous calls to the server, then provide live updates in the app by reading from a long-living server request.

Before starting to work on the app, start the book server. If you haven't already done that, navigate to the server folder **00-book-server** in the book materials-repository and enter swift run. The detailed steps are covered in Chapter 1, "Why Modern Swift Concurrency?".

Adding Functionality to Blabber

In the first section of this chapter, you'll work on finishing some missing app functionality. That will give you a solid start when you work on your own custom sequences in the following sections.

Go to **BlabberModel.swift**, where you'll add most of the app's logic throughout this and the following chapters. The chat() method in BlabberModel includes the code to open a long-living request that will return real-time updates.

> **Note:** Just as in previous chapters, "long-living" means the URL request doesn't time out. This lets you keep it open so you can constantly receive server updates in real time.

Once it establishes a connection, that method calls readMessages(stream:). This is the method you'll work on in this section.

Parsing the Server Responses

The custom chat protocol that the book server implements sends a status as the first line, then continues with chat messages on the following lines. Each line is a JSON object, and new lines appear whenever users add chat messages. This is all part of the same long-living request/response. Here's an example:

```
{"activeUsers": 4}
...
{"id": "...", "message": "Mr Anderson connected", "date": "..."}
...
{"id": "...", "user": "Mr Anderson", "message": "Knock
knock...", "date": "..."}
/// and so on ...
```

This is a bit different from what you've done in previous chapters — it requires more work to handle the response.

Scroll down to readMessages(stream:) and add this code to read the first line of the server response:

```
var iterator = stream.lines.makeAsyncIterator()

guard let first = try await iterator.next() else {
  throw "No response from server"
}
```

In the code above, you first create an iterator over the `lines` sequence of the response. Remember, the server sends each piece of data on a separate text line. You then wait for the first line of the response using `next()`.

> **Note**: Using an iterator and `next()` instead of a `for await` loop lets you be explicit about the number of items you expect to deal with. In this case, you initially expect one, and only one, server status.

Next, decode that server status by adding:

```
guard
  let data = first.data(using: .utf8),
  let status = try? JSONDecoder()
    .decode(ServerStatus.self, from: data)
else {
  throw "Invalid response from server"
}
```

Here, you convert the text line to `Data` and then try to decode it to a `ServerStatus`. The starter project includes a `ServerStatus` data model containing a single property called `activeUsers`. This is how the server tells you how many users are in the chat at the moment.

Storing and using the chat information

To store this information, add the following code immediately after the decoding:

```
messages.append(
  Message(
    message: "\(status.activeUsers) active users"
  )
)
```

`messages` is a published property on `BlabberModel` that contains the messages displayed onscreen. Most `Message` values are user messages posted in chat. They contain a specific user and date, but in this case, you use a convenience initializer that only accepts the message, as the initial status is considered a **system message**.

To use the server status you fetched, you create a new system message that says **X active users** and add it to the messages array.

After the initial status, the server sends an ever-growing list of chat messages, each on its own line.

This is similar to what you've done in previous chapters. You can abandon the iterator that you just used because the number of items you are expecting is now open-ended.

Next, move on to consuming the rest of the stream with a `for await` loop:

```
for try await line in stream.lines {
  if let data = line.data(using: .utf8),
    let update = try? JSONDecoder().decode(Message.self, from:
  data) {
    messages.append(update)
  }
}
```

You iterate over each response line and try to decode it as a `Message`. If the decoding succeeds, you add the new message to `messages`. Just like before, your UI will immediately reflect the change.

Now, the final piece of the app's core is in place. Build and run. Give Blabber a try by entering a user name and tapping the enter button on the right-hand side of the login screen:

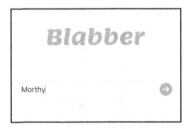

The app reads the first message from the server, then displays the server status at the top of the chat screen. Enter one or more messages in the text field at the bottom, then send them off to the server. You'll see them pop right back onscreen, meaning the server received them and then sent them back to you:

Don't be alarmed if some unexpected messages appear too, as in the screenshot above. This is just the chat bot Bottley trying to jump into the discussion.

When you get bored of talking to Bottley, who isn't the best conversationalist, you can launch more simulators and start a conversation between your alter egos, instead:

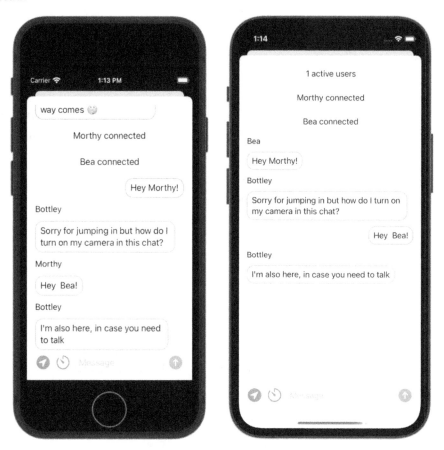

Well, look at that — you already have a somewhat functioning chat app at your fingertips. How cool!

Digging into AsyncSequence, AsyncIteratorProtocol and AsyncStream

In the previous section, you learned that an asynchronous sequence lets you access its elements via its iterator. In fact, defining the element type of the sequence and providing an iterator are the *only* requirements of the AsyncSequence protocol:

```
protocol AsyncSequence {
  ...
    func makeAsyncIterator() -> Self.AsyncIterator
}
```

There are no further requirements regarding *how* you produce the elements, no constraints on the type lifetime — nothing. In fact, quite the opposite: Open AsyncSequence's documentation (https://developer.apple.com/documentation/ swift/asyncsequence); you'll see that the protocol comes with a long list of methods, similar to those offered by Sequence:

```
func contains(_:) -> Bool
func allSatisfy(_:) -> Bool
func first(where:) -> Self.Element?
func min() -> Self.Element?
func max() -> Self.Element?
...
```

The iterator also powers for await loops, which you're probably already quite familiar with at this point.

You don't need to limit yourself to the most obvious use cases. Here are just a few examples of different sequences that you might easily create on your own:

By adopting AsyncSequence, you can take advantage of the default implementations of the protocol, for free: prefix(while:), contains(), min(), max() and so on.

The sequence's iterator must conform to `AsyncIteratorProtocol`, which is also very minimal. It has only one requirement — an `async` method that returns the next element in the sequence:

```
protocol AsyncIteratorProtocol {
  ...
  func next() async throws -> Self.Element?
}
```

Simple Asynchronous Sequences

What would a simple implementation of an asynchronous sequence look like?

Below is an example of a typewriter — an asynchronous sequence that "types" a phrase adding a character every second. Don't add this code to the project, just review it. If you really want to try it out — create a blank Xcode playground and try it there.

```
struct Typewriter: AsyncSequence {
  typealias Element = String

  let phrase: String

  func makeAsyncIterator() -> TypewriterIterator {
    return TypewriterIterator(phrase)
  }
}
```

The type has a `phrase` to type out, which you pass to the iterator. The iterator looks like this:

```
struct TypewriterIterator: AsyncIteratorProtocol {
  typealias Element = String

  let phrase: String
  var index: String.Index

  init(_ phrase: String) {
    self.phrase = phrase
    self.index = phrase.startIndex
  }

  mutating func next() async throws -> String? {
    guard index < phrase.endIndex else {
      return nil
    }
    try await Task.sleep(nanoseconds: 1_000_000_000)
```

```
        let result = String(phrase[phrase.startIndex...index])
        index = phrase.index(after: index)
        return result
    }
}
```

The iterator holds a copy of the string. Each time you call next(), it returns a substring of the initial string that is one character longer than the last one.

Finally, when it reaches the end of the phrase, either by a for await loop or some code that calls next() directly, next() returns nil to signify the end of the sequence.

> **Note**: If you're wondering why Task.sleep(nanoseconds:) is throwing — it throws a CancellationError if the current task is canceled while it's sleeping. Throwing an error is the quickest way to cleanly and safely wrap up the current execution without waiting the given amount of time.

You can now use this type like any other AsyncSequence:

```
for try await item in Typewriter(phrase: "Hello, world!") {
    print(item)
}
```

Which produces the following output, eventually:

```
H
He
Hel
Hell
Hello
Hello,
Hello,
Hello, w
Hello, wo
Hello, wor
Hello, worl
Hello, world
Hello, world!
```

As easy as creating a custom AsyncSequence is, it still requires you to add two extra types to your codebase.

To avoid clutter, you can make a single type conform to both AsyncSequence and AsyncIteratorProtocol, but there's also another, *much* easier, way.

Simplifying Asynchronous Sequences with AsyncStream

To streamline creating asynchronous sequences, Apple has added a type called AsyncStream. It conforms to AsyncSequence and produces values from a single closure, where you define the custom logic for your sequence.

This is a big win for decreasing complexity in your code, because you don't have to add additional sequence types.

AsyncStream inherits all the default behaviors of AsyncSequence and lets you easily create streams of values by using either of these two custom initializers:

- **init(_:bufferingPolicy:_:)**: Creates a new stream that produces values of the given type, by the given closure. Your closure can control the sequence via a structure called a **continuation**. Use this variant when you want to pass the continuation to existing, non-async code such as a completion handler or delegate.

- **init(unfolding:onCancel:)**: Creates a new stream that produces values by returning them from the unfolding closure. It optionally executes an onCancel closure when it's canceled. You would use this variant when wrapping async code as a sequence.

AsyncStream certainly allows for somewhat simpler async code. For example, to reproduce the typewriter example from earlier you'd write something like this:

```swift
var phrase = "Hello, world!"
var index = phrase.startIndex
let stream = AsyncStream<String> {
  guard index < phrase.endIndex else { return nil }
  do {
    try await Task.sleep(nanoseconds: 1_000_000_000)
  } catch {
    return nil
  }

  let result = String(phrase[phrase.startIndex...index])
  index = phrase.index(after: index)
  return result
}

for try await item in stream {
  print(item)
}
```

This code uses the `unfolding` variant of `AsyncStream`, where the iterator calls your closure and expects it to return each element in turn or `nil` to complete the sequence. Now that you know a bit about `AsyncStream`, you'll use it to build a countdown feature into Blabber.

Creating an Asynchronous Timer With AsyncStream

The countdown feature in the Blabber app adds an element of drama to your chats by counting down before showing your latest message.The countdown sequence won't do very much. It will start at three, count down to one before finally terminating with the user's message:

The first approach that might come to your mind is to use Apple's `Timer` type available in Swift. While this approach would have been sensible in the past, `Timer` carries a lot of baggage from the pre-async era that you don't want to deal with:

- You can only schedule a `Timer` on the main thread.

- `Timer`'s API doesn't accept an async closure.

- You have to code your own guarantees that it mutates variables safely.

Considering all of the above, in this chapter you'll implement a simple countdown using the new `async/await` syntax yourself.

Open **BlabberModel.swift** and scroll to `countdown(to:)`. The timer button in the UI calls this method when the user taps it. Right now, it's almost empty and ready for you to add some code.

Add this code at the bottom of the method:

```
var countdown = 3
let counter = AsyncStream<String> {

}
```

This creates an `AsyncStream` of the unfolding variant that produces `String` values. Inside the trailing closure, you'll add your own logic to produce those values.

Building Your Timer Logic

Now, you will build up the timer logic out of few simple steps. Insert this *inside* AsyncStream's trailing closure:

```
guard countdown >= 0 else { return nil }
```

Here, you check if your countdown variable is still greater than zero. Otherwise, you return nil to terminate the stream. This way the timer will stop counting down when it reaches zero.

Now, append this right after the previous line, still inside the stream closure:

```
do {
  try await Task.sleep(for: .seconds(1))
} catch {
  return nil
}
defer { countdown -= 1 }
```

On every timer tick, you put the task to sleep for one second and then decrease countdown. This is the core logic that drives the timer.

In case the current execution gets cancelled anywhere up the task hierarchy Task.sleep(for:) will throw, you will catch the error and return nil to terminate the stream. Easy as pie!

Finally, add the code to return each sequence value:

```
if countdown == 0 {
  return "🎉 " + message
} else {
  return "\(countdown)..."
}
```

If your timer has already completed you return the initial message the user wrote. In case you're still counting down, just return the current seconds left.

Build and run. Once you log in, enter something in the text field and tap the timer button:

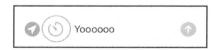

Nothing happens! Right now, your stream is producing values, but nobody's listening. The values will buffer until something consumes them.

To iterate over the values, add this code at the bottom of the method, outside any of the previous closures:

```
for await countdownMessage in counter {
  try await say(countdownMessage)
}
```

You call say(_:) for each of the values, which sends all the messages over to the server.

Build and run. Play through the timer routine and you'll see the completed message sequence:

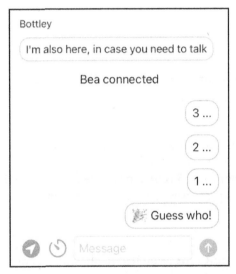

Next, you'll learn how to wrap existing closure-based asynchronous APIs as async sequences.

Adding an Asynchronous Stream to NotificationCenter

Going back and forth between closure-based asynchronous APIs and the modern async/await-based APIs can be tedious. Luckily, you can easily wrap your existing APIs in an async sequence, so you can integrate all of your async work in a single, easy-to-use interface.

In this section of the chapter, you'll try your hand at converting another system-provided API into an asynchronous sequence. Specifically, you'll add a method to `NotificationCenter` that lets you iterate over notifications in a `for await` loop:

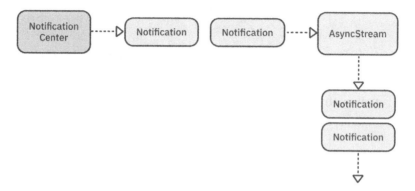

You'll use your new, asynchronous API to send messages like **user went away** and **user came back** to the server when the user closes or re-opens the app.

Note: Since writing this chapter, Apple added a built-in API to observe notifications asynchronously called `NotificationCenter.notifications(named:object:)`. Notifications remain, regardless, a great way for you to learn about wrapping synchronous APIs.

Open **Utility/NotificationCenter+.swift**. Inside, an empty extension declaration waits for you to add your new method to it. For this task you will use the second initializer overload of `AsyncStream` which allows you to use a continuation object to bridge sync and async APIs.

Add the following:

```
func notifications(for name: Notification.Name) ->
AsyncStream<Notification> {
  AsyncStream<Notification> { continuation in

  }
}
```

This method takes a notification name and returns an iterable, asynchronous stream.

Next, you'll observe the required notifications and use the `AsyncStream.Continuation.yield(_:)` method to add them to the stream.

Insert this code **inside** `AsyncStream`'s closure:

```
NotificationCenter.default.addObserver(
    forName: name,
    object: nil,
    queue: nil
) { notification in
    continuation.yield(notification)
}
```

Here, you observe the default center for notifications with the given name. Whenever one comes in, you pipe it through via `continuation.yield(_:)`. A notification stream is infinite, because there isn't a fixed number of notifications.

Now, open **BlabberModel.swift** and add a new method to observe the app status and post updates to the server:

```
func observeAppStatus() async {

}
```

Inside the method, add a `for await` loop to iterate over `willResignActiveNotification` notifications:

```
for await _ in NotificationCenter.default
    .notifications(for:
UIApplication.willResignActiveNotification) {

}
```

The system posts that notification when you switch to a different app or go back to your device's home screen and the current app isn't active anymore. Note how you use _ in the loop assignment because you aren't interested in the notification's details.

Notifying Participants When a User Leaves

To post a system message that the user has left the chat, add the following inside the loop you added at the end of the previous section:

```
try? await say("\(username) went away", isSystemMessage: true)
```

You call `say(_:)` as before, except you set the `isSystemMessage` to `true`. Because this is an automated message, you ignore any errors thrown from here.

Now, call `observeAppStatus()` just before you start the updates from the chat server. Scroll to `readMessages(stream:)` and insert this code *before* the `for await` loop:

```
let notifications = Task {
  await observeAppStatus()
}
```

This creates a new asynchronous task and starts observing for notifications. You store that task in the local `notifications` variable because — as you might have guessed already — you want to cancel the observation once the loop completes.

Immediately after the last few lines, add this code:

```
defer {
  notifications.cancel()
}
```

This will cancel your observation safely because the code in `defer` will run when either the `for await` loop throws or it completes successfully.

With that out of the way, it's time to test the notification sequence! Build and run. Log in, then:

1. Go to the home screen by clicking **Device ▸ Home** in the iOS Simulator menu or pressing **Command-Shift-H**.

2. Click **Device ▸ App Switcher** in the menu, then click **Blabber** to go back to the app. You can also simply find the Blabber icon on the simulator's home screen and tap it to go back to the app.

You'll see the **X went away** message on all connected simulators:

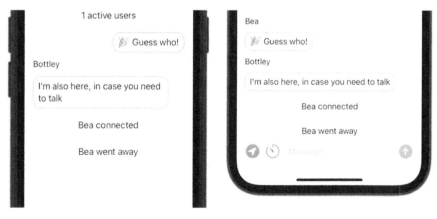

Now that you've notified your participants when a user leaves, it's time to let them know when users come back as well.

Notifying Participants When a User Returns

To wrap up this section, you'll also observe didBecomeActiveNotification to let the chat participants know when a user returns to the chat.

Scroll to observeAppStatus() and find the spot to add a second loop to observe for the additional notification.

Should you add the second for await loop *before* or *after* the first one? Since the code execution suspends for the duration of the loop, you can't do *either* — because one of the two loops will then have to wait for the other to complete.

The two loops need to run in parallel, so you have to wrap each one in a Task. Edit observeAppStatus() to run the two tasks in parallel, like so:

```
func observeAppStatus() async {
  Task {
    for await _ in NotificationCenter.default
      .notifications(for:
UIApplication.willResignActiveNotification) {
      try? await say("\(username) went away", isSystemMessage:
true)
    }
  }

  Task {
    for await _ in NotificationCenter.default
      .notifications(for:
UIApplication.didBecomeActiveNotification) {
      try? await say("\(username) came back", isSystemMessage:
true)
    }
  }
}
```

Build and run one more time. Repeat the same test routine as the last time.

Your code handles both notifications and there are two system messages, one for when you leave the app and another when you come back:

Extending AsyncSequence

Extending existing types is not an async/await feature per se, but with AsyncStream being so simple to use, your attention might stray away from the possibilities of extending the concrete AsyncStream type or even the more generic AsyncSequence protocol.

Apple maintains an open source repository with common async algorithms you can use right out of the box with your async sequences: https://github.com/apple/swift-async-algorithms. The package offers handy, commonly used implementations of debounce, throttle, merge, zip, and more.

If you're coming to async/await from a Combine or an RxSwift codebase, definitely check out this package as it will make your transition much more straightforward.

In this section, you'll add a new method to `AsyncSequence` to make iterating over sequences more readable in some cases.

The Swift `Sequence` protocol features a handy convenience method called `forEach(_:)` that runs the given closure for each of the sequence's elements. You'll add the same method to `AsyncSequence` so you can use `forEach(_:)` instead of the `for await` loop.

`forEach(_:)` comes in handy when your code uses multiple sequence methods in succession to process the elements, like so:

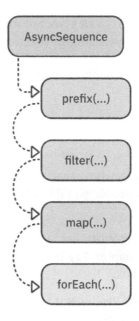

The implementation is so simple that you'll add it directly in **BlabberModel.swift**.

At the bottom of the source file, after any of the existing declarations, add:

```
extension AsyncSequence {
  func forEach(_ body: (Element) async throws -> Void) async
throws {

  }
}
```

In this new extension, you add a method to *all types* that conform to `AsyncSequence`, which takes an asynchronous, throwing closure and returns no result.

Next, add the implementation inside the new method:

```
for try await element in self {
  try await body(element)
}
```

You asynchronously iterate over the sequence values and, as soon as any of them is available, pass it to `body(_:)`.

Now, you have your own extension to *all* asynchronous sequences. If at times you feel like `for await` is too wordy, you can use `forEach` instead.

To try the new method, scroll to `countdown(to:)` and replace the `for await` loop with:

```
try await counter.forEach {
  try await say($0)
}
```

Arguably, the code isn't much less wordy than the `for await` loop. However, in case `say(...)` had only the one parameter, you'd be able to use it simply as: `try await counter.forEach(say)`.

It's time to congratulate yourself! With that last addition to the project code, you've finished working through this chapter. `AsyncStream` is one of the most powerful tools in your `async/await` toolbox.

If you had fun bridging existing APIs like `NotificationCenter`, you'll *love* the next chapter, where you'll learn how to bridge *any code* with the special **continuation** APIs.

Key Points

- You can use **iterators** and **loops** to implement your own processing logic when consuming an AsyncSequence.

- AsyncSequence and its partner in crime, AsyncIteratorProtocol, let you easily create your own asynchronous sequences.

- AsyncStream is the easiest way to create asynchronous sequences from a single Swift closure.

- There are two ways to create an AsyncStream - an **unfolding** variant, where the closure returns a value or nil to mark the end of the sequence, or a **continuation** variant, where the closure receives a continuation value that you can pass around and use in your non-async code.

Chapter 5: Intermediate async/await & CheckedContinuation

By Marin Todorov

In the previous chapter, you worked through creating custom asynchronous sequences. At this point, you should already feel right at home when it comes to using `AsyncSequence` and `AsyncStream`.

You saw that wrapping existing APIs, like `NotificationCenter`, is very powerful, letting you reuse your tried-and-tested code in your modern async/await codebase.

In this chapter, you'll continue working in the same direction. You'll look into more ways to reuse existing code to the fullest by leveraging Swift's superpowered concurrency features.

Introducing Continuations

Two patterns of asynchronous programming have dominated Apple platforms for a long time: callbacks and the delegate pattern. With completion callbacks, you pass in a closure that executes when the work completes. With the delegate pattern, you create a delegate object, then call certain methods on it when work progresses or completes:

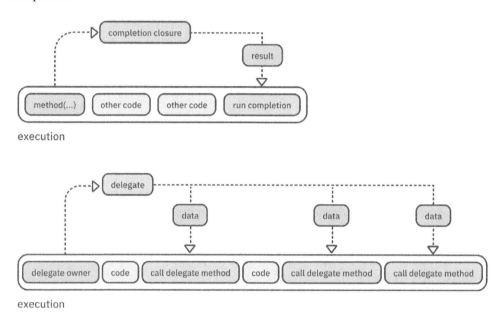

To encourage the new concurrency model's adoption, Apple designed a minimal but powerful API that comes in handy when bridging existing code. It centers around the concept of a **continuation**.

A continuation is an object that tracks a program's state at a given point. The Swift concurrency model assigns each asynchronous unit of work a continuation instead of creating an entire thread for it. This allows the concurrency model to scale your work more effectively based on the capabilities of the hardware. It creates only as many threads as there are available CPU cores, and it switches between continuations instead of between threads, making the execution more efficient.

You're familiar with how an `await` call works: Your current code **suspends** execution and hands the thread and system resources over to the central handler, which decides what to do next.

When the awaited function completes, your original code resumes, as long as no higher priority tasks are pending. But how?

When the original code suspends, it creates a continuation that represents the entire captured state at the point of suspension. When it's time to resume execution or throw, the concurrency system recreates the state from the continuation and the work... well, *continues*.

```
func hello() async throws -> String {
    try await Task.sleep(nanoseconds: 1_000_000)
    return "Hello world"
}                              resume

                                                    suspend
let result = try await hello()
print(result)
```

This all happens behind the scenes when you use `async` functions. You can also create continuations yourself, which you can use to extend existing code that uses callbacks or delegates. These APIs can benefit from using `await` as well.

Manually creating continuations allows you to migrate your existing code gradually to the new concurrency model.

Creating Continuations Manually

There are two continuation API variants:

1. **CheckedContinuation**: A mechanism to resume a suspended execution or throw an error. It provides runtime checks for correct usage and logs any misuse.

2. **UnsafeContinuation**: An alternative to `CheckedContinuation`, but without the safety checks. Use this when performance is essential and you don't need the extra safety.

> **Note**: The APIs are essentially identical, so you'll only work with `CheckedContinuation` in this chapter. For any function mentioned in this chapter that has "checked" in its name, you can assume there's an "unsafe" equivalent as well.

You don't normally initialize a continuation yourself. Instead, you use one of two handy generic functions that take a closure. The closure provides a ready-to-use continuation as an input parameter:

- **withCheckedContinuation(_:)**: Wraps the closure and gives you a checked continuation back.

- **withCheckedThrowingContinuation(_:)**: Wraps a throwing closure. Use this when you need error handling.

You **must** resume the continuation once — and exactly once. Enforcing this rule is the difference between checked and unsafe continuations. You resume a continuation by using one of the following ways:

- **resume()**: Resumes the suspended task without a value.

- **resume(returning:)**: Resumes the suspended task and returns the given value.

- **resume(throwing:)**: Resumes the suspended task, throwing the provided error.

- **resume(with:)**: Resumes with a `Result` containing a value or an error.

The methods above are the only ones you can call on a continuation, which is yet another easy-to-use, minimal type.

Next, you'll wrap `CLLocationManagerDelegate` to learn how to quickly use continuations to reuse your existing code.

Wrapping the Delegate Pattern

In this chapter, you'll continue working on the Blabber project, starting where you left off at the end of the last chapter. Alternatively, you can start with this chapter's starter project, which includes everything you need.

Start the book server now, if you haven't already. Navigate to the server folder in the book materials-repository, **00-book-server**, and enter `swift run`. The detailed steps are covered in Chapter 1, "Why Modern Swift Concurrency?".

Some APIs use the delegate pattern to continuously "talk" to their delegate — for example, to send progress updates or notifications about app state changes. When you need to handle multiple values, you should use an `AsyncStream` to bridge the delegate pattern to newer code.

In other cases, like in this chapter, you'll need to handle a single delegation callback or a completion — and that's the perfect opportunity to use a continuation!

In the next few sections, you'll focus on letting the users share their location in chat:

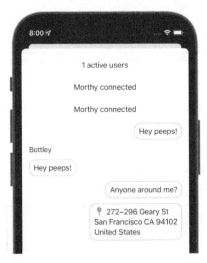

When you work with location data, you need to reach out to one of the oldest frameworks in iOS: `CoreLocation`.

Note: Offering apps that were capable of providing location-based services was one of the iPhone 2's killer features — and one of the reasons why it became a huge success. `CoreLocation` is one of the frameworks that iOS 2 initially made available to third-party developers.

As a *classic* API, `CoreLocation` heavily relies on delegates, making it a perfect candidate for you to learn how to interoperate between `async/await` code and those older patterns.

The main type you usually deal with in the `CoreLocation` framework is `CLLocationManager`. When you ask this type to start location updates, it repeatedly calls its delegate with the current device location:

execution

In Blabber, you don't want to share the user location continuously, but only once — when the user taps the location button. You'll create your own location delegate type and code the logic to fetch the user's coordinates.

Open **BlabberModel.swift** and scroll to `shareLocation()`. This method is already wired to the location button in the chat screen:

Managing the Authorizations

You'll get started by creating a location manager and verifying that the user has authorized the app to use the device location data.

Before dealing with any `CoreLocation`-specific work, add the following code that creates a continuation:

```
let location: CLLocation = try await
withCheckedThrowingContinuation { [weak self] continuation in

}
```

`withCheckedThrowingContinuation(_:)` takes a throwing closure, suspends the current task, then executes the closure. You should call your asynchronous code from within the closure, then resume the `continuation` argument when you're done. In this case, you'll resume with an error or a location.

You can pass `continuation` around like any other variable, storing it in your model or passing it over to other functions. Wherever it ends up, calling one of its `resume(...)` methods will always resume the execution at the original call site.

Also, you might have noticed that the function contains "checked" in its name. That indicates the **runtime** checks if you use the continuation safely.

Build and run the project. Log in and tap the location button. You won't see an error onscreen. However, look at the Xcode console output, and you'll see the following, between other logs:

```
SWIFT TASK CONTINUATION MISUSE: shareLocation() leaked its
continuation!
```

The runtime detected that you never used `continuation` and that the variable was released at the end of the closure. Long story short, your code at `try await withCheckedThrowingContinuation(...)` will never successfully resume from its suspension point.

As mentioned earlier, you *must* call a `resume(...)` method exactly once from each code path.

Next, you'll fix this by integrating your `continuation` with a newly minted delegate.

Building up the Location Manager

Open **Utility/ChatLocationDelegate.swift**, where you'll find the placeholder type `ChatLocationDelegate`. Notice that all the `CLLocationManagerDelegate` requirements are optional, so the file compiles without any of `CLLocationManagerDelegate`'s methods.

You'll add two methods to handle location updates and location errors.

First of all, inside the class definition, add a new type alias for a throwing continuation that returns a location:

```
typealias LocationContinuation = CheckedContinuation<CLLocation,
Error>
```

That alias name will make your code a little less verbose.

Since your delegate holds on to the continuation until it receives a location, you need to store it in a property. Add the property, like shown below:

```
private var continuation: LocationContinuation?
```

You also need a new initializer so you can **inject** the continuation and also ask the location manager for the needed permissions. Add that next:

```
init(manager: CLLocationManager, continuation:
LocationContinuation) {
  self.continuation = continuation
  super.init()
  manager.delegate = self
  manager.requestWhenInUseAuthorization()
}
```

First of all, note the use of `super.init()`; this lets you set `self` as the location manager's delegate *before* requesting authorization.

Then, you call `requestWhenInUseAuthorization()` to show the system privacy dialogue, which sets the authorization status on the manager object. If the user has already granted permissions, the method does nothing. You'll deal with the various authorization values later in the chapter.

> **Note**: You'll need to grant location permissions to continue with this chapter. If you denied location usage by mistake, or you wanted to test what happens if you rejected the permissions, don't worry — just delete the app from the iOS Simulator. The next time you run the project, you'll get the authorization dialogue again.

The first delegate method you need is the one that gets called when the location permissions update. This happens when the permissions have been granted and immediately after the location manager is created. Add the following delegate method to `ChatLocationDelegate`:

```
func locationManagerDidChangeAuthorization(_ manager:
CLLocationManager) {
  switch manager.authorizationStatus {
  case .notDetermined:
    break
  case .authorizedAlways, .authorizedWhenInUse:
    manager.startUpdatingLocation()
  default:
    continuation?.resume(
      throwing: "The app isn't authorized to use location data"
    )
    continuation = nil
  }
}
```

If the user hasn't responded to the permissions request, which would happen the first time they run the app, you do nothing. If they've granted the permissions, you tell the location manager to start getting location data. Otherwise, you'll resume the continuation with an error.

After resuming, you destroy the continuation because doing anything else with it is illegal.

Next, add the delegate method that's called when the user's location updates:

```
func locationManager(
  _ manager: CLLocationManager,
  didUpdateLocations locations: [CLLocation]
) {
  guard let location = locations.first else { return }
  continuation?.resume(returning: location)
  continuation = nil
}
```

The locations argument contains a list of CLLocation values. Here, it's safe to take the first one and pass it on to your own code.

Additionally, you call continuation?.resume(returning:) to resume the original code execution and return the first location from the suspension point:

```
                                                              resume
let location: CLLocation = try await withCheckedThrowingContinuation { continuation
..........................................................    ..............................

    func locationManager(_ manager: CLLocationManager,
        didUpdateLocations locations: [CLLocation]) {

        guard let location = locations.first else { return }
        continuation?.resume(returning: location)
        continuation = nil
    }
```

Finally, just like before, you set the continuation property to nil.

Next, add error handling via locationManager(_:didFailWithError:):

```
func locationManager(
  _ manager: CLLocationManager,
  didFailWithError error: Error
) {
  continuation?.resume(throwing: error)
  continuation = nil
}
```

If the manager fails to fetch the device location, it calls this method on its delegate so you can update your app accordingly.

You use `continuation?.resume(throwing:)` to resume your original code at the suspension point and throw the given error:

```
                                              throw
    let location: CLLocation = try await withCheckedThrowingContinuation { continuation
    . . . . . . . . . . . . . . . . . . . . . . . . . . . . . . . . . . . . . . . . . .
    func locationManager(_ manager: CLLocationManager,
        didFailWithError error: Error) {

        continuation?.resume(throwing: error)
        continuation = nil
    }
```

At the end, as you did before, you set `continuation` to `nil` to release the continuation you just used.

You now have the complete workflow in place: Once you set up the location manager with the delegate, it will try to fetch the current location and will call one of the methods you've wired to use the injected `continuation`:

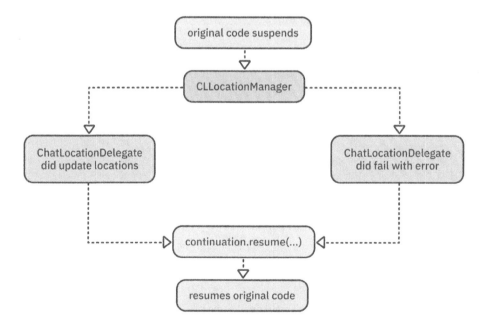

Additionally, when the continuation resumes, you reset `continuation` so you can't use it more than once.

This concludes the setup. After having made use of async/await in the last few chapters, do you already feel like delegates are a drag? That's not unreasonable — delegates can make solving some simpler tasks a lot more verbose than they need to be.

Now, it's time to start the updates and set the whole machinery in motion.

Using Your Delegate

Open **BlabberModel.swift** again and add these two properties to the class:

```
private let manager = CLLocationManager()
private var delegate: ChatLocationDelegate?
```

The first one is the location manager, which you will reuse whenever the user taps the location button. The latter is the location delegate which you will recreate each time you need to fetch the user's location.

Then, in shareLocation() inside the closure of withCheckedThrowingContinuation(_:), insert the following:

```
self?.delegate = ChatLocationDelegate(manager: manager,
continuation: continuation)
if manager.authorizationStatus == .authorizedWhenInUse {
  manager.startUpdatingLocation()
}
```

You just created a ChatLocationDelegate and injected the continuation you got from withCheckedThrowingContinuation(_:) to it. You store the resulting delegate to a predefined delegate property to make sure it isn't immediately released from memory.

After that, what happens is:

1. The manager calls the change authorization delegate method when it initializes.

2. After the user grants permissions, the manager fetches the device location.

3. The manager calls the delegate with an array of CLLocations.

4. The delegate calls continuation and resumes by returning the first available CLLocation.

5. The original call site let location: CLLocation = try await withCheckedThrowingContinuation ... resumes execution, letting you use the returned location value.

To test the result, append the following code at the very bottom of the function, after `withCheckedThrowingContinuation`:

```
print(location.description)
manager.stopUpdatingLocation()
delegate = nil
```

When the process completes, you'll see the location object printed in Xcode's console. Finally, you stop the location updates and reset `delegate` because you don't need it anymore, once you get a location.

Build and run. Tap the location button to give the new feature a try.

There could be two outcomes of this. You will either see a location printed in the output console if you've used Xcode to simulate location data in the past. Alternatively, you will see an error like so:

By the way — how *cool* is that?

You didn't write any special code to handle the error — you pipe in the error from your delegate, then your `continuation` re-throws it. Finally, you catch the error seamlessly in the button action. For the last mile, the starter SwiftUI code updates `lastErrorMessage` on the chat view, which pops the alert box onscreen.

There's a small wrinkle here though, which exposes a useful learning opportunity. If you don't enable location simulation, the location manager only throws an error the first time you ask it for a location. This means that if you ask for a location again, the manager does not call its delegate methods, which means your continuation will never resume.

You can try this out by tapping the location button again in the chat window, making sure you haven't turned on location simulation from Xcode. If you are seeing a location in the console, switch to another simulator or reset the one you are working on. You will see the console error about leaking the continuation that you saw earlier.

What's happening? When you tap the location button, a new delegate is created, and the old one is destroyed. This takes the continuation with it, and the continuation has not been resumed, which is against the rules. You could possibly see something like this in real-world use if you hit the button multiple times before a location fix was obtained.

To make absolutely sure the continuation always resumes, open **ChatLocationDelegate.swift** and add the following code to ChatLocationDelegate:

```
deinit {
  continuation?.resume(throwing: CancellationError())
}
```

Throwing a cancellation error is the standard way to say that your async code can stop doing its work. You probably don't want to display this in an alert, though, so open **ChatView.swift** and find the code that calls model.shareLocation(). Above the catch block, add the following code to catch and ignore cancellation errors:

```
} catch is CancellationError {
  // Ignore cancellation errors.
```

This will prevent cancellation errors being displayed to the user. After that brief diversion, you can get back to location handling. If you haven't tested location-aware apps in Xcode before, you need to enable location data in the iOS Simulator.

At the bottom of the code editor in Xcode, click the location button and pick one of the default locations in the list:

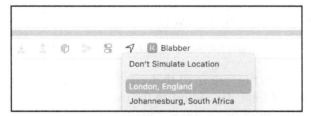

Once you're feeding location data successfully into the iOS Simulator, you'll see the location icon fill with color:

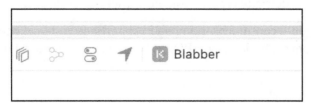

Log in again and tap the location button. This time, you'll see the coordinates of your selected location in the console:

```
<+19.01761470,+72.85616440> +/- 5.00m (speed -1.00 mps / course
-1.00) ...
```

Great work so far! You've gone through setting up a continuation and creating a proxy delegate. Now, you can apply this approach in basically any scenario.

To exercise this routine one more time, you'll look into wrapping up a callback-based API next.

Wrapping Callback APIs With Continuation

In the system frameworks that Apple introduced after iOS 4, most asynchronous APIs are callback-based.

That means that when you call a given method, you provide a parameter with a closure that executes asynchronously when the method finishes its work.

For example, if your app wants to request authorization to provide parental controls, you need to call
`AuthorizationCenter.requestAuthorization(completionHandler:)` from Apple's **FamilyControls** framework, like so:

```
AuthorizationCenter.shared
  .requestAuthorization { result in

  }
```

Calling this API displays the system UI that asks for authorization, if necessary. After an arbitrary amount of time, depending on the user's actions, it calls back to your closure. It returns the authorization status via the `result` closure argument.

Having a single closure is arguably a little easier to wrap with a continuation than creating a separate delegate type, as you did earlier in the chapter.

In this section, you'll continue working on `BlabberModel.shareLocation()` by wrapping a custom callback-based API that turns a location into a human-readable address.

The Blabber starter project includes a custom type called `AddressEncoder`. It converts a location to a human-readable address via a classic callback API: `AddressEncoder.addressFor(location:completion:)`.

In this section, you'll work through calling that API and using a continuation to make it fit seamlessly with the rest of your asynchronous code.

Creating the Closure

Open **BlabberModel.swift** and scroll back to the method called `shareLocation()`, where you added your delegate wrapping code.

To make the new call to `AddressEncoder`, add this code at the bottom of `shareLocation()`:

```
let address: String = try await
withCheckedThrowingContinuation { continuation in

}
```

You start this section the same way that you approached wrapping `CLLocationManager`'s delegate — by calling `withCheckedThrowingContinuation(_:)` to create a closure with a continuation to control asynchronous execution.

This time, you'll return a `String` when you resume. That string will be the human-friendly address for the location coordinates you already have.

Now, insert this code inside the closure:

```
AddressEncoder.addressFor(location: location) { address, error
in

}
```

Here, you call `addressFor(location:completion:)`. In the completion callback, you receive an optional address and an optional error.

This is, unfortunately, a common pattern in Swift APIs, especially before the official introduction of the `Result` type.

This pattern opens the code for undesired scenarios — for example, when the closure receives both a nil result and a nil error...

You'll have to make the best of the situation and try resuming with the correct behavior for each callback outcome. Add this switch inside the callback closure from above:

```
switch (address, error) {
case (nil, let error?):
  continuation.resume(throwing: error)
case (let address?, nil):
  continuation.resume(returning: address)
}
```

You switch over address and error:

• When you get an error, you pipe it through to the continuation via continuation.resume(throwing:).

• On the other hand, if you get an address back, you return it via continuation.resume(returning:).

So far, so good — but the compiler now complains that you need to handle *all* the possible combinations.

Add two more cases inside the switch statement to handle any unexpected callback input:

```
case (nil, nil):
  continuation.resume(throwing: "Address encoding failed")
case let (address?, error?):
  continuation.resume(returning: address)
  print(error)
```

• If you get nil for both the address and the error, that's clearly some kind of unknown error, so you throw a generic error: **Address encoding failed**.

• If you get both an address *and* an error, you return the address — but also print the error so that the message remains in the app's log.

That clears the compiler error, and you cover all the bases when it comes to unexpected callbacks from AddressEncoder.

> **Note**: If you already peeked into the source code of `AddressEncoder`, you know that it will never call the completion closure with incorrect parameters. However, you can't do that for APIs where you don't have access to the source code. That's why it's important to handle invalid API usage defensively.

It's time for the final line in `shareLocation()`. After your new `withCheckedThrowingContinuation`, append:

```
try await say("📍 \(address)")
```

Once you have the address as a string, you call `BlabberModel.say(_:)` to share it in chat.

Build and run one more time. Enable location simulation in Xcode and tap the location button in the app:

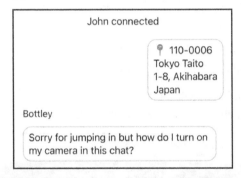

With that last addition to the Blabber app, you've covered most of the continuation APIs, and you've used continuations to bridge delegates and callbacks. Doing this will allow your `async/await` code to work *alongside* your existing codebase, not *against* it.

You'll continue working with Blabber in the next chapter, where you'll learn more about debugging and testing your asynchronous code.

If you'd like to work through one more exercise, stay around for this chapter's optional challenge.

Challenges

Challenge: Build a Command-line Version of Blabber

This is an *optional* challenge that you can try on your own to exercise some of the concepts of the last few chapters.

In this challenge, you'll build the Clipper app: a CLI (Command Line Interface) version of Blabber. It lets you grab a user name and chat with friends from a Terminal window.

In the introduction section of Chapter 1, "Why Modern Swift Concurrency?", you covered platform restrictions for Swift concurrency features. As a reminder, you're building a macOS app here. That means that if you're using Xcode 13.2 or newer, you can run this challenge on macOS 10.15 or later. If you're using an earlier version of Xcode 13, you have to be running macOS 12.

This project's twist is that, as a command-line app, it's an exercise in creating a complete chat app in about 30 lines of code.

When you've successfully completed the challenge, you'll be able to open multiple Terminal windows and chat between your alter egos.

Open the starter challenge project for this chapter by double-clicking **Package.swift**. The Clipper app consists of a single source file called **main.swift**.

Inside, you'll find:

- A long-living `URLSession` for live updates called `liveURLSession`.

- One `Task` that accesses the `/cli/chat` server endpoint. Its job is to print the chat messages.

- A second `Task` that iterates over the standard user input and sends any messages the user enters to the server.

Believe it or not — that's the complete chat app!

You can try completing the code on your own; if you prefer the guided tour, however, follow these steps:

1. Inside the do block in the first `Task`, get a `bytes` stream of the `url` address defined in the task. Then, iterate over the lines, like you did in previous chapters, and print each line. Use `liveURLSession` so the request doesn't time out.

That's all! To test the chat, follow these steps:

- Start the book server.

- Open multiple Terminal windows.

- In each window, change the current directory to the Clipper folder — the folder containing **Package.swift**.

- In each window, type `swift run Clipper [username]` and replace [username] with the chat name you'd like to use.

- You'll see a message from the server confirming you're connected: [username connected].

- Now, you can chat by entering messages in each Terminal.

Key Points

- You bridge older asynchronous design patterns to `async/await` by using `CheckedContinuation` or its unsafe counterpart, `UnsafeCheckedContinuation`.

- For each of your code paths, you need to call one of the continuation's `resume(...)` methods **exactly once** to either return a value or throw an error.

- You get a continuation by calling either `withCheckedContinuation(_:)` or `withCheckedThrowingContinuation(_:)`.

Chapter 6: Testing Asynchronous Code

By Marin Todorov

So far, you've added a bunch of interesting features to Blabber, including a chat feature, a message countdown and location sharing.

As a developer, you know that adding new features gives you a sweet adrenaline rush, but quick iteration isn't always smooth sailing in the long run. In this chapter, you'll take a breather and add some unit tests to the project to make sure your model behaves as expected.

Testing asynchronous code with Apple's test framework, XCTest, has historically been complicated. Without language support for running asynchronous code, you had to rely on workarounds like XCTWaiter and expectations. Additionally, you had to wait until the test under code was complete before you could verify its output.

From what you've learned so far in this book, you might think you need to do something complicated to make an asynchronous context within your testing code. Luckily, you don't! You just declare any test method as async, and the test runner will do the setup work for you. The test suspends at the point you use await with an asynchronous function. Once it resumes, you can verify the output as usual:

test execution

As you see in the diagram above, the new syntax lets you write asynchronous tests linearly, *as if* they were synchronous. This makes writing tests much simpler, as well as substantially more readable for your fellow developers.

> **Note**: You will see that the improvements to XCTest are rather minimal. Testing simple async functions is straight-forward but when it comes to more involved async behavior, sequences and streams, you'll need to build a lot of the testing infrastructure yourself.

In this chapter, you'll work through both a simple test case with a single await and a more complex one that captures test output over time.

Capturing Network Calls Under Test

Open the starter version of Blabber in this chapter's materials, under **projects/ starter**. Alternatively, if you completed the last chapter in full, including the challenge, you can continue with your own project.

Next, open **BlabberTests.swift**, where you'll add your tests for the BlabberModel type. So far, there are no tests. No bueno!

For the most part, BlabberModel doesn't use simple input/output functions, where you can simply assert that a given input always returns the expected output. Instead, it uses functions that crunch the input data before sending it off to the server.

The full chain of events looks like this:

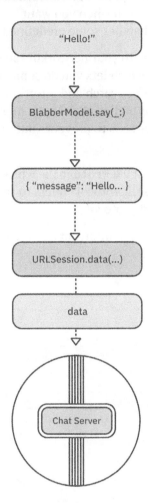

Your goal now is to add asynchronous tests to verify that BlabberModel always sends correct data to the server.

Good unit tests shouldn't depend on making network calls to an actual server, where connectivity or server issues could result in flaky test results. There are two common approaches to testing networking calls:

- Injecting a **mock URLSession-like type** that captures requests on your tests' behalf.

- Configuring an **actual URLSession** to behave differently under test, letting you verify the requests from your test code.

In this chapter, you'll work through the second option. Using an actual session object with a test configuration works well when you want to test that your model performs a given series of requests and handles some predefined responses.

You'll add custom URL handlers to your networking stack via URLSession.configuration, which lets you do some nifty things. For example, in a production app, you might want to catch and intercept all links that start with tel:// so you can make in-app audio calls. Or you might custom-handle URLs starting with https://youtube.com to prevent your users from switching to the YouTube app.

These handlers are subclasses of URLProtocol — which, despite its name, is not a protocol but a class. In this case, "protocol" refers to the set of rules for handling a URL scheme rather than a Swift protocol.

For your tests in this chapter, you'll intercept and record *all* network requests using a custom URLProtocol subclass:

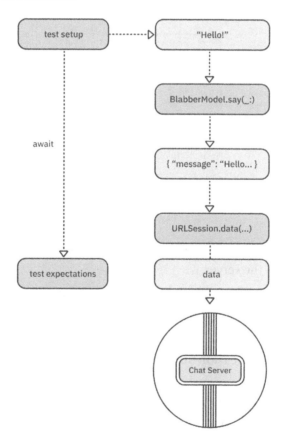

Implementing a Custom URLProtocol

Open **Utility/TestURLProtocol.swift**. Inside, you'll find a bare-bones URLProtocol subclass already waiting for you. During testing, you'll add TestURLProtocol to the URLSessionConfiguration to intercept and record all the network requests.

The minimum protocol requirements, which are already included in the code, are:

- **canInit(with:)**: Returns true when the current protocol should handle the given URLRequest. In this case, you always return true since you want to catch *all* requests.

- **canonicalRequest(for:)**: This method can alter requests on the fly. In this case, you simply return the given request with no changes.

- **startLoading()**: Here, you load the request and send a response back to the client.

- **stopLoading()**: Call this method when the operation is canceled or when the session should otherwise stop the request. For these tests, you don't have to add anything here.

The starter code in startLoading() creates a successful server response with no content and returns it to the client. For these tests, you're only interested in the outgoing requests, not what comes back from the server. You'll also record the network requests here.

Next, add this new property to the TestURLProtocol type:

```
static var lastRequest: URLRequest?
```

Each time TestURLProtocol responds to a request, you'll store it in lastRequest so you can verify its contents.

You probably noticed that the property is static. Because of the way you pass these URL protocols to URLSessionConfiguration, you can't easily access instance properties, as you'll see in a moment. For the simple tests in this chapter, this will do just fine.

Next, add the code to store each request at the bottom of `startLoading()`:

```
guard let stream = request.httpBodyStream else {
  fatalError("Unexpected test scenario")
}

var request = request
request.httpBody = stream.data
Self.lastRequest = request
```

In this block, you take several steps:

- First, you verify that the request has a non-`nil` `httpBodyStream` input stream. That's the stream you use to read the request data.

- You make a new mutable `request` variable so you can modify the request before storing it.

- You read the request contents from `httpBodyStream` and store the data in `httpBody`.

- Finally, you save the request in `lastRequest` so your tests can verify the contents after the network call completes.

That's all it takes to complete your custom catch-all URL protocol. Now, you just need to use it to spy on what your app is sending.

Creating a Model for Testing

Switch back to **BlabberTests.swift** and add a new property in `BlabberTests`:

```
@MainActor
let model: BlabberModel = {
  // 1
  let model = BlabberModel()
  model.username = "test"

  // 2
  let testConfiguration = URLSessionConfiguration.default
  testConfiguration.protocolClasses = [TestURLProtocol.self]

  // 3
  model.urlSession = URLSession(configuration:
testConfiguration)
  return model
}()
```

The property is annotated with @MainActor to ensure BlabberModel is isolated to the main actor. You'll learn more about that in Chapter 8. Here's what the code above does:

1. Create a new BlabberModel with the given username.

2. Create a URL session configuration that uses TestURLProtocol to handle URL requests.

3. Tell the model to use this new session.

TestURLProtocol will handle all the network calls made by this instance of BlabberModel so you can inspect them in your tests.

Now, it's time to write a test!

Adding a Simple Asynchronous Test

A critical point to remember when adding asynchronous tests is to add the async keyword to each test method. Doing this lets you await your code under test and easily verify the output.

Add the following method to BlabberTests to create your first test:

```
func testModelSay() async throws {
  try await model.say("Hello!")

}
```

Since the model is already configured to use the test-suitable URL session, you don't need to do any additional setup — you just call say(_:) right away.

At this point, you're ready to add your test expectations. First, you'll verify that the last request the network performed, model.say("Hello!"), was sent to the correct URL.

Add the following code to do that:

```
let request = try XCTUnwrap(TestURLProtocol.lastRequest)

XCTAssertEqual(
  request.url?.absoluteString,
  "http://localhost:8080/chat/say"
)
```

You first unwrap the optional TestURLProtocol.lastRequest, then check that the URL matches the expected address: http://localhost:8080/chat/say.

Now that you've verified that the model sends the data to the correct endpoint, you can check that it also sends the correct data.

Finish up your test with the following piece of code:

```
let httpBody = try XCTUnwrap(request.httpBody)
let message = try XCTUnwrap(try? JSONDecoder()
  .decode(Message.self, from: httpBody))

XCTAssertEqual(message.message, "Hello!")
```

You expect request.httpBody to decode as a Message. Once decoded, you assert that the message text equals **"Hello!"**, as expected.

If you wrote asynchronous tests prior to Swift 5.5, you're likely excited about the brevity and clarity of this test code. And if you haven't written asynchronous tests before, you really don't need to know the lengths you had to go to set up a good asynchronous test back then!

To run the test, click **Play** in the editor gutter, to the left of func testModelSay()..., or press **Command-U** to run all tests.

Regardless of how you go about it, you'll see the test **pass** and a green check mark (the best check mark!) will appear next to the test name in Xcode:

```
46
       func testModelSay() async throws {
48         try await model.say("Hello!")
49
50         let request = try XCTUnwrap(TestURLProtocol.lastRequest)
51
```

Testing Values Over Time With AsyncStream

Now that you've created a test that awaits a single value, you'll move on to testing asynchronous work that may yield *many* values.

Start by adding another test to **BlabberTests.swift**:

```
func testModelCountdown() async throws {

}
```

As you already guessed, this test verifies if `BlabberModel.countdown(to:)` behaves as expected.

This time around, you're in for a much more complex testing scenario, so be prepared to brace!

> **Note**: Some tests are simply more challenging to design than others. If a given piece of code is difficult to test, that usually means you can improve the code itself — for example, by breaking it down into logical pieces and making it more composable. But sometimes, depending on the situation, tests are just complex. However, you'll see that using `async/await` makes even complex tests easier to design.

Your `say(_:)` test was fairly simple because the method does a single thing and only sends a single network request:

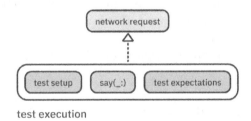

countsdown(to:), in comparison, is more involved. It sends up to four network requests, so you can't verify only the last one in the sequence to guarantee the method works correctly:

This is really *nice* for you because it gives you the opportunity to use some of the new modern concurrency APIs.

Switch back to **TestURLProtocol.swift**. There, you store the last accepted request in lastRequest. Now, you'll add a new function that returns a **stream of all requests**. You'll then be able to call countdown(to:) and verify all the requests it sent.

To start, add the following code to TestURLProtocol:

```
static private var continuation:
AsyncStream<URLRequest>.Continuation?

static var requests: AsyncStream<URLRequest> = {
  AsyncStream { continuation in
    TestURLProtocol.continuation = continuation
  }
}()
```

This code adds a static property holding a continuation as well as a new static property, requests, which returns an asynchronous stream that emits requests.

Inside the requests getter you create a new AsyncStream and store its continuation. Note that, since continuation is a static property, you can have only one active instance of requests at a time.

You need to store the continuation so you can emit a value each time TestURLProtocol responds to a request. This is easy to handle — you just add a didSet handler to lastRequest.

Replace the lastRequest property declaration with this code:

```
static var lastRequest: URLRequest? {
  didSet {
    if let request = lastRequest {
      continuation?.yield(request)
    }
  }
}
```

Now, updating lastRequest will also emit the request as an element of the asynchronous stream that requests returns.

Great, these are all the changes you need to make in TestURLProtocol!

Completing the Countdown Test

Switch back to **BlabberTests.swift** and scroll to testModelCountdown(). It's time to finally add your test code.

Add this code to `testModelCountdown()`:

```
try await model.countdown(to: "Tada!")
for await request in TestURLProtocol.requests {
  print(request)
}
```

Here's what the code above is doing:

1. Make a call to `countdown(to:)`.

2. Iterate over the stream of requests to print the recorded values.

Run the test by clicking **Play** in the editor gutter:

```
     func testModelCountdown() async throws {
69       try await model.countdown(to: "Tada!")
70       for await request in TestURLProtocol.requests {
71         print(request)
72       }
73     }
74   }
```

Let the test run for a while... sadly, the execution never completes. The logs in Xcode's output console prove that the test is hanging:

```
Test Suite 'Selected tests' started at 2021-09-02 13:53:33.107
Test Suite 'BlabberTests.xctest' started at 2021-09-02
13:53:33.108
Test Suite 'BlabberTests' started at 2021-09-02 13:53:33.109
Test Case '-[BlabberTests.BlabberTests testModelCountdown]'
started.
```

As per the last log message, the test runner started `testModelCountdown`, but it never completed.

Next, add breakpoints on all three of the lines you just added and run the test again to verify where the execution stops:

```
     func testModelCountdown() async throws {
69       try await model.countdown(to: "Tada!")
70       for await request in TestURLProtocol.requests {
71         print(request)
72       }
73     }
74   }
```

The debugger stops on the first and second lines, but it never hits the breakpoint on `print(request)`. The stream never emits any values.

What's going on here? Look back at how you emit the requests: You only emit values when `lastRequest` is set. When your test starts the `for await` loop, `countdown(to:)` has already finished, so there are no requests to read.

It seems like you'll have to scrap the current code and take a new approach. There's one *essential* thing you should notice during this exercise:

`await` **does not time out**!

That means that if some of the tested code doesn't behave correctly, your tests will just **hang forever** at some `await` suspension point.

This is not a problem with your test, *per se.* `await` simply doesn't time out at all. If that turns into a problem in your code, you can fix this by adding some custom code to cancel your task if it takes longer than expected to complete.

You'll take a quick detour from finishing `testModelCountdown()` and do just that — add the supporting infrastructure to your tests so they safely time out, instead of hanging forever.

Adding TimeoutTask for Safer Testing

You can't let your tests hang indefinitely — that would defeat the purpose of verifying incorrect behavior. Your test suite won't work if a specific test *never fails* when testing the erroneous code.

In this section, you'll create a new type called `TimeoutTask`. This type is similar to `Task` except that it will throw an error if the asynchronous code doesn't complete in time.

In the **Utility** folder inside **BlabberTests**, create a new file called **TimeoutTask.swift**.

Since you'll use that file in your tests, take a moment after creating it to double-check that it only belongs to your test target. You can verify this under the **Target Membership** section in the File inspector on the right-hand side of the Xcode window while you have **TimeoutTask.swift** open:

If you haven't checked the checkbox next to **BlabberTests**, do so now. Next, replace *all* of the code in your new file with:

```
import Foundation

class TimeoutTask<Success> {

}

extension TimeoutTask {
  struct TimeoutError: LocalizedError {
    var errorDescription: String? {
      return "The operation timed out."
    }
  }
}
```

Here, you create a new type that is generic over `Success`, just like Swift's `Task` is. `Success` is the type of result the task returns, if any. If the task doesn't return a result, then `Success` is `Void`. Additionally, you define a `TimeoutError`, which you'll throw if the task times out.

With the basic setup out of the way, you can add the initializer for `TimeoutTask`, too, along with some useful properties:

```
let seconds: Int
let operation: @Sendable () async throws -> Success

init(
  seconds: Int,
  operation: @escaping @Sendable () async throws -> Success
) {
  self.seconds = seconds
  self.operation = operation
}
```

The first parameter of your new initializer is the maximum duration in seconds. The second parameter is `operation`, which is (deep breath…) an escaping, thread-safe, asynchronous, throwing closure. To go through all of those keywords:

- **@escaping**: Indicates that you may store and execute the closure outside of the initializer's scope.

- **@Sendable**: You can't conform to protocols for closures or function types in the same way that you can with other types. This new keyword indicates that a closure or function type conforms to the `Sendable` protocol, meaning it's safe to transfer between concurrency domains.

- **async**: Hopefully, you're familiar with this term by now. It means the closure should execute in a concurrent asynchronous context.

- **throws**: The closure can throw an error.

That's a cumbersome set of keywords, but they all help the compiler and the runtime clearly understand your intentions and run your code correctly.

The initializer doesn't do anything other than storing its values. Here, it differs from Task, which starts executing immediately.

> **Note**: You'll learn more about the Sendable protocol and the @Sendable annotation for function parameters in Chapter 8, "Getting Started With Actors".

Starting the Task and Returning its Result

Next, you'll add a property called value, which will start the work and asynchronously return the result of the task. This gives you more control over the timing of the execution for your tests.

Add the following code to TimeoutTask:

```
private var continuation: CheckedContinuation<Success, Error>?

var value: Success {
  get async throws {
    try await withCheckedThrowingContinuation { continuation in
      self.continuation = continuation
    }
  }
}
```

As you've done in previous chapters, you declare the value getter as async and throws so you can control execution asynchronously.

Inside the getter, you start by calling withCheckedThrowingContinuation(_:) to get a continuation. This lets you either complete successfully or throw an error if the operation times out.

Once you get the initialized continuation, you store it in the instance property called continuation.

To start implementing the execution logic, add this task immediately after storing the continuation, while still in `withCheckedThrowingContinuation`'s closure:

```
Task {
    try await Task.sleep(for: .seconds(seconds))
    self.continuation?.resume(throwing: TimeoutError())
    self.continuation = nil
}
```

Here, you start an asynchronous task that sleeps for the given number of seconds — the timeout duration you use when creating a `TimeoutTask`. You then use the stored `continuation` to throw a `TimeoutError()`.

So far, so good — you've implemented the part of the code that times out. Now, immediately after the previous `Task`, add the code that does the actual work:

```
Task {
    let result = try await operation()
    self.continuation?.resume(returning: result)
    self.continuation = nil
}
```

In this asynchronous task, you execute the initial `operation` closure. If that completes successfully, you use `continuation` to return the result.

You start two asynchronous tasks in parallel and let them race towards the final. Whichever task completes first gets to use the `continuation`, while the slower task gets canceled.

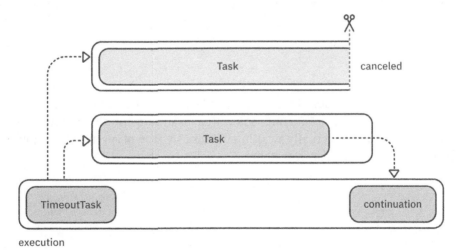

> **Note**: On a rare occasion, it's possible that both tasks might try to use
> continuation at *precisely* the same time — leading to a crash. You'll learn
> about Swift's actor type and writing safe concurrent code in later chapters.
> For now, leave the TimeoutTask code as-is.

Canceling Your Task

To wrap up your new type, you'll add one more method: cancel(). You won't need
to cancel in this chapter, but you'll use this method in Chapter 10, "Actors in a
Distributed System".

Inside TimeoutTask, add:

```swift
func cancel() {
  continuation?.resume(throwing: CancellationError())
  continuation = nil
}
```

The new method uses the stored continuation and throws a
CancellationError(), like Apple's own asynchronous APIs do when they're
canceled.

To try your new task, switch back to **BlabberTests.swift** and wrap the for await
loop inside testModelCountdown() in a TimeoutTask, so it looks like this:

```swift
try await TimeoutTask(seconds: 10) {
  for await request in TestURLProtocol.requests {
    print(request)
  }
}
.value
```

As before, you call countdown(to:) and then iterate over requests — but this time,
you wrap the latter inside a TimeoutTask with a maximum duration of ten seconds.
You'll also notice you're actually awaiting the task's value property, which holds all
of the timeout logic you just worked on.

If you still have breakpoints on the test suite, turn them off. Then, run
`testModelCountdown()` one more time. After a while, you'll see the test fail:

```
67
⊗      func testModelCountdown() async throws {          ◇   caught error: "The operation timed out."
69        try await model.countdown(to: "Tada!")
70        try await TimeoutTask(seconds: 10) {
71          for await request in TestURLProtocol.requests {
72            print(request)
73          }
74        }
75        .value
76      }
77    }
```

Congratulations, you now have your own `Task` alternative that allows you to write
safer asynchronous tests!

Sadly, this indisputable victory does not resolve your initial problem. Even though
the test doesn't hang anymore, it still fails. And, to finally be able to ship your
progress into your (hypothetical) code repository, your tests need to pass.

Using async let to Produce Effects and Observe Them at the Same Time

If you remember, the reason the test hangs is that the operations take place in order,
and the countdown finishes before you start reading the stored request stream.

You already learned how to start multiple asynchronous tasks and execute them in
parallel in Chapter 2, "Getting Started With async/await." You need to make multiple
`async let` bindings and await them all. That's what you'll do in this test.

Replace the contents of `testModelCountdown()` one last time with:

```
async let countdown: Void = model.countdown(to: "Tada!")
```

Since `countdown(to:)` doesn't return a value, you need to explicitly define the
binding type as `Void`. You'll use `countdown` in a while to await the countdown
method along with the task that will observe the recorded network requests.

Now, for the second binding:

```
async let messages = TestURLProtocol.requests
```

If you think about it, you don't really need all the elements in `requests`. You only need as many as you expect during a successful run of `countdown(to:)`. That means you need four requests, one for each message sent to the server.

Simply add this as the next line, just like you would for a regular Swift sequence:

```
.prefix(4)
```

Because you expect four requests, you take only four elements in the sequence. Now, add the following below:

```
.compactMap(\.httpBody)
.compactMap { data in
  try? JSONDecoder()
    .decode(Message.self, from: data)
    .message
}
```

In this code, you:

- Grab `httpBody` from each of the requests, if it's available.

- Try to decode the body as a `Message`.

- Return the `message` property as the result.

Finally, to collect the expected four messages into an array, add one more function call:

```
.reduce(into: []) { result, request in
  result.append(request)
}
```

`reduce(...)` runs the given closure for each element in the sequence and adds each request to `result`. Now you have, as result, a simple plain array.

Long story short, you collect all the text messages in the messages array, like so:

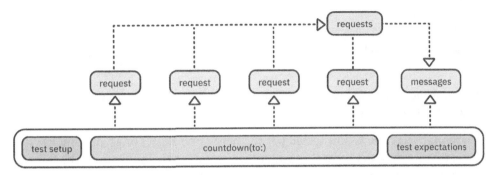

test execution

The code, however, still hangs if you only get three requests instead of the expected four. The execution will stop at prefix(4) and wait for a fourth element.

You need to wrap your messages binding in a TimeoutTask, so messages ends up looking like this:

```
async let messages = TimeoutTask(seconds: 10) {
  await TestURLProtocol.requests
    .prefix(4)
    .compactMap(\.httpBody)
    .compactMap { data in
      try? JSONDecoder()
        .decode(Message.self, from: data).message
    }
    .reduce(into: []) { result, request in
      result.append(request)
    }
}
.value
```

With the two bindings ready, the only thing left to do is await them concurrently and verify the output.

Add the following line to await the messages:

```
let (messagesResult, _) = try await (messages, countdown)
```

You don't care about the result of countdown, so you only store messagesResult.

Finally, verify the contents of `messagesResult`:

```
XCTAssertEqual(
  ["3...", "2...", "1...", "🎉 Tada!"],
  messagesResult
)
```

Run `testModelCountdown()` once more. This time around, it passes with a green check mark. Fantastic work!

Even though the code is now tested per se, there's one aspect of asynchronous testing that might quickly turn into a problem as your test suite grows. The two unit tests that you just added take over five seconds to complete!

Who has the time to wait for hundreds or thousands of such tests?

Speeding up Asynchronous Tests

For both synchronous and asynchronous tests, you often need to inject mock objects that mimic some of your real dependencies, like network calls or accessing a database server.

In this last section of the chapter, you'll inject a "time" dependency in `BlabberModel` so that time goes a little faster when you're running your tests. Namely, you will use a mock alternative of `Task.sleep` so that `Blabber.countdown(to:)` doesn't need to spend so much time waiting.

Open **BlabberModel.swift** and add a new property, where you'll store the sleeping function that the model should use:

```
var sleep: (Int) async throws -> Void = {
  try await Task.sleep(for: .seconds($0))
}
```

In the code above, you define a new property called `sleep` and set its default value to `Task.sleep(for:)`. Next, scroll to `countdown(to:)` and insert the following at the top:

```
let sleep = self.sleep
```

You can use the local copy of the function to do the "sleeping" you'll need a few lines later.

Now, replace the `try await Task.sleep(for: .seconds(1))` line with:

```
try await sleep(1)
```

Now, your model behaves *exactly the same way* as before by default. But you can easily override the `sleep` property in your tests to change the speed at which the code sleeps.

Updating the Tests

To wrap up, you'll update the tests next. Open **BlabberTests.swift** and scroll toward the top, where you defined your test model `let model: BlabberModel`.

After the line where you inject the test URL session, `model.urlSession`, append this line:

```
model.sleep = { try await Task.sleep(for: .nanoseconds($0)) }
```

Your test implementation of `sleep` takes the parameter passed to the function and instead of suspending for the given amount of seconds — it suspends for the given amount of *nanoseconds*! This should certainly speed up things.

Effectively, you still implement the same workflow as before and provide the same suspension point at the right moment in the execution. The only difference is that you run the code a billion times faster.

Run the tests one more time by pressing **Command-U** and check the duration. Now, you can keep growing your test suite without worrying about how much time it's going to take to run all the tests!

With `async`/`await` and the modern concurrency APIs, designing asynchronous tests becomes much easier. Nevertheless, the design of your tests depends *mostly* on the code under test. Since your code will vary in nature, you'll always need to create some slightly different setups and conduct tests somewhat differently.

In this chapter, you covered different situations and worked on building your own testing infrastructure. You're now ready to write asynchronous tests in your own apps.

Key Points

- Annotate your test method with `async` to enable testing asynchronous code.

- Use `await` with asynchronous functions to verify their output or side effects after they resume.

- Use either **mock types** for your dependencies or the **real type**, if you can configure it for testing.

- To test time-sensitive asynchronous code, run **concurrent tasks** to both trigger the code under test and observe its output or side effects.

- `await` can suspend indefinitely. So, when testing, it's a good idea to set a **timeout** for the tested asynchronous APIs whenever possible.

Chapter 7: Concurrent Code With TaskGroup

By Marin Todorov

You've made your way through a lot of new concepts so far. At this point, you're hopefully comfortable with designing code with async/await, creating asynchronous sequences and running tasks in parallel with async let bindings.

async let bindings are a powerful mechanism to help design your asynchronous flow, especially when you have a mix of tasks where some need to run in parallel, while others depend on each other and run sequentially.

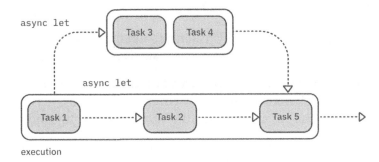

While you have *some* flexibility to decide how many and which tasks to run with async let, that syntax doesn't offer *truly* dynamic concurrency.

Imagine that you need to run a thousand tasks in parallel. Writing async let a thousand times is out of the question! Or what if you don't know in advance how many tasks you need to run in parallel, so you need to write code that can handle that decision at runtime?

Luckily, there's a solution: meet `TaskGroup`, the modern API that allows you to create dynamic concurrency in your code. `TaskGroup` is an elegant API that allows you to create concurrency on the fly, reduces the possibility of data races and lets you safely process the results.

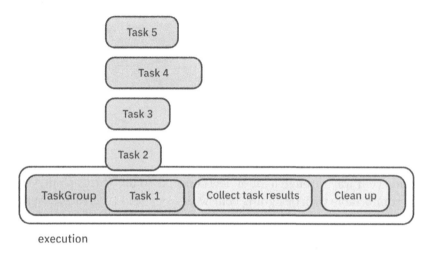

execution

Introducing TaskGroup

As in previous chapters, you'll start by reading a short overview of the APIs you'll try. You'll then move on to working on a brand new, aliens-related project!

There are two API variants used to construct a task group: `TaskGroup` and `ThrowingTaskGroup`. Like other APIs you've covered in this book, these two variants are almost identical. The difference is that the latter allows for throwing tasks.

You don't initialize a task group yourself — as both APIs don't offer public initializers. Instead, you use one of the following handy generic functions, which creates a group for you and assists the compiler in properly type checking your code:

- **withTaskGroup(of:returning:body:)**: Creates a group with the given task return type, the given return type for the final result you'll construct from tasks in the group, and the body closure as the code that initializes and runs the group.

- **withThrowingTaskGroup(of:returning:body:)**: Takes similar parameters, but each task, as well as the group as a whole, might throw an error.

An important point about these functions is that they *only* return once the group finishes running all of its tasks.

Here's a short example that demonstrates how to use a task group:

```
//1
let images = try await withThrowingTaskGroup(
  of: Data.self
  returning: [UIImage].self
) { group in
  // 2
  for index in 0..<numberOfImages {
    let url = baseURL.appendingPathComponent("image\
(index).png")
    // 3
    group.addTask {
      // 4
      return try await URLSession.shared
        .data(from: url, delegate: nil)
        .0
    }
  }
  // 5
  return try await group.reduce(into: [UIImage]()) { result,
data in
    if let image = UIImage(data: data) {
      result.append(image)
    }
  }
}
```

Don't be put off if the code doesn't speak to you at first. Like most modern concurrency APIs, this example is both your first encounter with `TaskGroup` and almost everything you need to know about it.

Step by step, this code does the following:

1. You set each task's return type as `Data` via the `of` argument. The group as a whole will return `[UIImage]`. You could also have an explicit return type in the closure declaration and skip the `returning` argument.

2. Elsewhere in your code, you've calculated the number of images you want to fetch, which lets you loop through them here.

3. `group` is the ready-to-go `ThrowingTaskGroup`. Inside the `for` loop, you use `group.addTask { ... }` to add tasks to the group.

4. You perform the actual work of the task by fetching data from an API.

5. Task groups conform to your old friend `AsyncSequence`, so as each task in the group completes, you collect the results into an array of images and return it.

Long story short, the example starts a variable number of concurrent tasks, and each one downloads an image. Finally, you assign the array with all the images to `images`. Those few lines of code really pack quite a punch!

execution

You manage the group's tasks with the following APIs:

- **addTask(priority:operation:)**: Adds a task to the group for concurrent execution with the given (optional) priority.

- **addTaskUnlessCancelled(priority:operation:)**: Identical to `addTask(...)`, except that it does nothing if the group is already canceled.

- **cancelAll()**: Cancels the group. In other words, it cancels all currently running tasks, along with all tasks added in the future.

- **isCancelled**: Returns `true` if the group is canceled.

- **isEmpty**: Returns `true` if the group has completed all its tasks, or has no tasks to begin with.

- **waitForAll()**: Waits until all tasks have completed. Use it when you need to execute some code after finishing the group's work.

As you see, `TaskGroup` conforms to `AsyncSequence`, so you can iterate over the group asynchronously to get the task return values, just like a regular Swift `Sequence`.

This is quite an ingenious design because it both runs concurrent tasks and iterates over the results as a sequence — and, therefore, in a non-concurrent context. That allows you to update your mutable state safely — for example, by storing the result of each task in an array.

In the next section, you'll try many of these great APIs in an app that searches for aliens.

Getting Started With Sky

In this chapter, you'll work on an iOS app called **Sky** that scans satellite imagery of the sky and analyzes it for signs of alien life.

You'll scan the numbered sectors in a satellite image independently from each other. This allows you to use TaskGroup and perform many of these scans in parallel.

> **Note:** The app will only *pretend* to scan the images. The goal of this chapter is to walk you through using concurrent task groups. If you're interested in *really* searching for alien life, check out The SETI Institute (https://bit.ly/3C4k62y).

As with other projects in the book, **Sky** consists of a single screen already built for you in SwiftUI. Most of your work will go into the app's model, which will spawn concurrent tasks and manage their execution.

To get started, open this chapter's starter project. Then, build and run it. You'll see the main app UI. It features three indicators that show the scheduled tasks, the current tasks-per-second ratio and the number of completed scans:

Tap the **Engage systems** button. The app will pop an alert telling you that it successfully scanned twenty sectors within zero seconds.

As you've already guessed, the app didn't *actually* perform anything. The button calls the starter code, but the model doesn't scan any data. That's why you get the record 0.00-second duration to complete the work.

The main points to note in the starter code are:

1. The scanModel property in **Sky/SkyApp.swift** is the initialized model. It takes the number of tasks to perform in a single run and the name of the local device. You'll use that name in a later chapter.

2. In **Sky/ScanModel.swift**, the three @Published properties that drive your UI are scheduled, countPerSecond and completed. onScheduled() and onTaskCompleted(), which you'll call from your own code later, manage those properties.

3. Finally, peek in **Sky/Tasks/ScanTask.swift**. This is the type that "performs" a sky-sector scan. It takes an input, which is the number of the sector, and performs the actual work in run(). Luckily for your computer, run() only *simulates* hard work by blocking its thread for one second. The fact that the task takes a known amount of time to run can help you confirm that you're running code in parallel.

Now that you've had a quick walkthrough of the project, you'll move on to implementing the part of the model that runs the scans.

Spawning Tasks in a Simple Loop

Open **ScanModel.swift** and add the following convenience method anywhere inside the ScanModel class:

```swift
func worker(number: Int) async -> String {
  await onScheduled()

  let task = ScanTask(input: number)
  let result = await task.run()

  await onTaskCompleted()
  return result
}
```

This method not only runs a single task, but also tracks the execution in the model's state. Here's what this code does:

- Call onScheduled() to update the model counters. This method is annotated with @MainActor because it updates the UI. Updating the UI should always be a fast operation, so the await here won't affect the progress of the scanning task significantly.

- Create a new ScanTask with the given sector number.

- Wait for the results of the asynchronous call to run().

- Finally, call onTaskCompleted() to update the model counters and the app's UI on the main thread once again.

onScheduled() and onTaskCompleted() are both annotated with @MainActor to guarantee that updating the model counters, even from multiple copies of worker(number:) running in parallel, is safe.

main thread

Next, scroll to runAllTasks(). The **Engage systems** button calls this method when you tap it. You'll add the code to perform concurrent scans here.

Now, add this code inside runAllTasks(). If you see a problem with the code, congratulate yourself, but indulge me and use it anyway:

```
var scans: [String] = []
for number in 0..<total {
  scans.append(await worker(number: number))
}
print(scans)
```

Here, you create an empty array called scans, then run a for loop to append the result of each scan task. Finally, you print the result to the console.

Build and run. Tap **Engage systems**; the indicators will liven up.

As the app progresses, you'll notice that there's always one scheduled task, and you're progressing at about one task per second.

If you've already noticed the flaw, this won't surprise you. You await the tasks *serially* inside the for loop instead of running in parallel.

Finally, when the scan completes, the app shows a duration of just over twenty seconds.

Each call to worker(number:) blocks the next one, regardless of whether the dispatcher uses one or more threads:

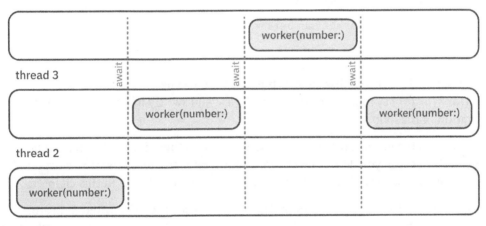

You need to work on multiple threads *at the same time* to perform concurrent work. You could do that manually by wrapping the code inside the loop in a Task. This would start all iterations immediately and at the same time.

But fear not, there's no need for manual labor. That's what the TaskGroup APIs do for you: launch tasks concurrently, track execution and, finally, collect the results.

Creating a Concurrent Task Group

Inside `runAllTasks()`, delete everything except the first line that resets `started`. Insert this instead:

```
await withTaskGroup(of: String.self) { [unowned self] group in

}
```

You use `withTaskGroup(of:operation:)` to create and run a task group. You also set each of the tasks to return a `String`. You'll call `worker(number:)` from inside the closure, so you capture `self` as an unowned reference.

Now, you can add some tasks to `group` by inserting this code in the `withTaskGroup(...)` closure:

```
for number in 0..<total {
  group.addTask {
    await self.worker(number: number)
  }
}
```

Here, you add a `for` loop like before, but this time you use `addTask(priority:operation:)` to add a task and swiftly move on to the next iteration of the loop.

Each task in the group calls `worker(number:)` and returns its result. This happens implicitly because you don't need to write `return` for single-expression closures. At the moment, you don't collect the task results, but you will later in this chapter.

Build and run. Tap **Engage systems**. This time, you see the **Scheduled** indicator shoot straight up to twenty — and then nothing happens for a while. Finally, the jobs complete.

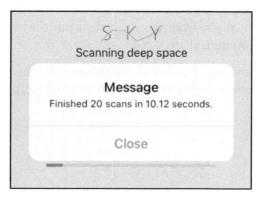

Note: You'll see a different completion time depending on how many execution threads the system has made available to your app. In the screenshot above, the work finished in about 10 seconds, which means the app used two threads. A duration of about 7 seconds would mean you were given three threads and so on. In the current version of the Xcode Simulator, only one execution thread is available. This means you will see the app finish in 20 seconds or more. If you'd like to observe concurrent work in action, you have to test on a device.

You'll deal with the lack of UI updates shortly, but something is definitely going right — the time it takes to complete all of the tasks dropped, meaning the app is now working concurrently!

The app has performed twenty seconds of work in ten seconds of actual time. This is your first hint that you're doing concurrency right — you're using more CPU time than the amount of astronomical time that's passed.

The duration is 50% shorter, and that means that the Swift runtime allotted two execution threads *at a time* from the thread-pool to your task group like so:

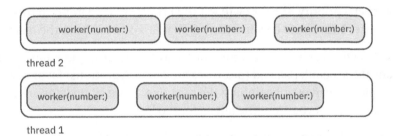

Because addTask(...) returns immediately, all twenty tasks are scheduled instantly, before the tasks start. The runtime then starts all the tasks, so the Scheduled indicator fills all the way up. Then, things start to go wrong. The work is being done, and being done concurrently, but you don't see any UI updates. Why is that?

Controlling Task Execution

Remember that the concurrency system breaks operations down into partials. Resuming after an await is a partial, just like anything else. After the first ScanTask.run() completes, the concurrency system now has to choose between running a different scheduled scan task or resuming any of the completed ones.

> **Note**: If you need a quick refresher on partial tasks in Swift, take a moment to review the section called "Separating code into partial tasks" in Chapter 2, "Getting Started With async/await".

You haven't given the system any information about which option is more important, so it's doing what you asked it to do first — running the scans.

Your users are anxious for news of alien life! To make the concurrency system understand this, you need to tell it that scanning tasks are less important than updating the UI.

Open **Sky/Tasks/ScanTask.swift** and update run() to give the task a priority.

Replace:

```
await Task {
```

With:

```
await Task(priority: .medium) {
```

If you don't set a priority, the task will get the priority of its parent. In this case, that priority is .userInitiated because the original task started from the main thread.

With this change, you give the scanning task a lower priority — medium, in this case. That means the scheduler *should* (priorities are only suggestions) favor resuming after a completed scan over beginning the next one. Since UI updates are super quick, this won't keep you from the aliens for too long.

Keep in mind that changing the priority here will *not make* tasks run faster or slower. It just bumps the UI tasks toward the front of the executor queue instead of appending them after all of the scan tasks.

Build and run. Tap **Engage systems**. Now, you'll see the completed progress fill up in real time:

With that wrinkle out of the way, you can return to figuring out if you found any alien life during this particular scan.

Getting Results From a Task Group

An important detail to note about withTaskGroup is that it waits for all tasks to finish before returning. That means that, on the next line of code after calling this function, it's safe to assume all the tasks have completed.

"But where is the *result* of the group execution?" you might ask. Since you don't explicitly return a value from withTaskGroup(...)'s trailing closure, the function returns no value (i.e., Void).

As you briefly touched upon earlier in the chapter, TaskGroup and ThrowingTaskGroup expose their results via an AsyncSequence conformance. In other words, you can use everything you already know about asynchronous sequences to iterate over the task results in group.

Open **ScanModel.swift** and scroll to runAllTasks(). At the end of the task group closure, after the for loop, add the following code:

```
return await group
  .reduce(into: [String]()) { result, string in
    result.append(string)
  }
```

You use reduce(into:block:), inherited from AsyncSequence, to collect all the returned task values and collect them in an array.

The compiler will promptly complain about this change. To fix that, update the line that creates the task group to add a closure return type and assign the result to a local variable, like so:

```
let scans = await withTaskGroup(
  of: String.self
) { [unowned self] group -> [String] in
```

This will clear the compiler error and also assign the group result to scans. To verify the group results, add the following **at the end** of the runAllTasks() method:

```
print(scans)
```

Build and run one more time. Tap **Engage systems** and, once the scanning completes, look at Xcode's output console. You'll see the values returned by the group:

```
["1", "0", "2", "3", "4", "5", "6", "7", "9", "10", "8", "11",
"13", "12", "15", "14", "16", "17", "18", "19"]
```

Note how the numbers aren't sorted in increasing order. TaskGroup executes tasks in the order it finds fitting to optimize system resources.

Additionally, tasks with higher priority will execute before tasks with lower priority, regardless of the order you add them.

Mutating Shared State

A final point to make about using task groups is that it's quite important to understand which parts of your code actually run **in parallel**.

> **Note**: The section below is relevant only when testing on a real device, as testing in the Simulator doesn't run code concurrently.

By design, you can return any results of the concurrent execution from the task and safely collect those results by iterating over the group. However, sometimes you need to update some kind of shared state directly from inside a group task.

For example, concurrent tasks that download a file from a server might log the result immediately via a shared app logger object. This way, if one of the files fails to download and the request throws an error, the rest of the requests will still log successfully as soon as they get the file:

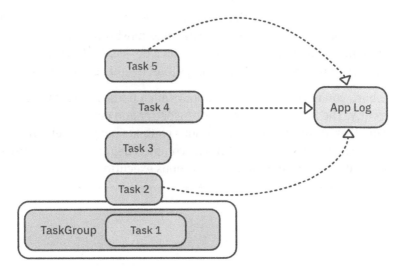

If you end up mutating shared state — like an instance property or a top-level variable — concurrently, you'll create a data race that might eventually crash your app. A data race occurs when multiple threads access the same data in memory, and at least one of them is trying to modify that data:

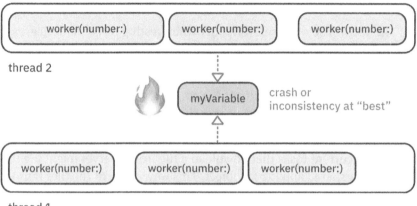

The tricky part about data races is that you *almost never* experience a crash when you run your app in debug mode from Xcode. Data races most often produce crashes when you compile an app to release and run it on a device. And as luck has it, it's bound to happen more often to your end users than to you as a developer.

Long story short, you need to be vigilant about which parts of your task group code run concurrently. The Swift compiler is getting better and better at preventing you from mutating shared state from asynchronous contexts but it's useful if you also had a good idea what exactly goes down. The completed group code roughly splits across concurrent, asynchronous and synchronous execution, like so:

```
let scans = await withTaskGroup(of: String.self) { [unowned self] group -> [String] in
  for number in 0..<total {                        asynchronous
    group.addTask {
      await self.worker(number: number)
    }                                  concurrent
  }
  return await group
    .reduce(into: [String]()) { result, string in
      result.append(string)
    }                                              asynchronous
}
print(scans)  synchronous
```

- It's **mostly safe** to modify shared state from the synchronous parts of the code (in green) — for example, from outside the task group.

- It's **somewhat safe** to modify state from asynchronous parts (in orange), if the compiler doesn't complain. But to do that, you have to be sure you aren't introducing a data race.

- It's **dangerous** to modify state from the concurrent parts (in red), unless you use a safety mechanism.

Luckily, the new concurrency model also provides a new API to make your concurrent code safe. You'll learn about it in detail in Chapter 8, "Getting Started With Actors".

At the moment, your group churns through all its tasks and eventually ends up with a result. But what if you were to actually find alien life? Wouldn't you want to do something about that right away? In the next section, you'll learn how to handle task results as they come in.

Processing Task Results in Real Time

Sometimes, you need to run a bunch of concurrent tasks and simply use the collected results at the end of the job, just as you implemented `runAllTasks()` in the previous section.

In other situations, you need to react immediately to each task's result. For example, you might want to update the UI to show progress or control the group execution flow depending on the task's results.

Luckily, `TaskGroup` allows you to **dynamically** manage the workload of the group. You can cancel tasks, add new tasks during execution and more.

> **Note**: This is an important distinction to make for readers who've used the older Grand Central Dispatch API in the past, `DispatchQueue.concurrentPerform(iterations:execute:)`, which didn't allow any control over the execution.

In the previous section, you collected the results and returned a value from
withTaskGroup. Now, you'll remove the return and process the results inside the
closure.

Open **ScanModel.swift**, if you don't already have it onscreen, and remove this entire
return statement from the closure in runAllTasks():

```
return try await group
    .reduce(into: [String]()) { result, string in
      result.append(string)
    }
```

To satisfy the compiler, change the task group creation code to account for the lack
of return value:

```
await withTaskGroup(of: String.self) { [unowned self] group in
```

Then remove this line, as well:

```
print(scans)
```

Now — on to the new code. At the bottom of withTaskGroup's closure, after the for
loop, append this:

```
for await result in group {
  print("Completed: \(result)")
}
print("Done.")
```

group conforms to AsyncSequence so you can comfortably iterate its results in a
loop.

The loop runs as long as there are pending tasks and suspends before each iteration.
It ends when the group finishes running all its tasks.

Build and run. Tap **Engage systems** and observe the output console. You'll see
something like:

```
...
Completed: 13
Completed: 14
Completed: 15
Completed: 17
Completed: 16
Completed: 19
Completed: 18
Done.
```

The runtime executes the tasks asynchronously. As soon as each task completes, the `for await` loop runs one more time.

Next, you'll look into gaining even more control over the group execution by using custom iteration logic.

Controlling the Group Flow

As mentioned earlier in the chapter, the `TaskGroup` APIs are very flexible, largely thanks to their simplicity. This section will show you how to combine these simple APIs to compose a more complex behavior.

Right now, you schedule all the tasks and let the runtime decide how many to execute and when, until it exhausts the tasks in the group. This, however, might not always be what you want to do.

Scanning for signs of alien life requires plenty of heavy work that might strain the device. In this section, you'll restrict the concurrent task group to execute **no more than four tasks** at the same time, making sure the Sky app never overloads your system.

> **Note**: Naturally, 20 tasks aren't going to overload an iPhone device. But think about systems where you have an infinite amount of tasks that could be dynamically fed into a work queue and/or distributed for execution across multiple devices. In such situations you'd like to only pull as much work as you plan to do and take on more tasks only when you complete the ongoing ones.

Scroll to `runAllTasks()` in **ScanModel.swift**, if you don't have it open at the moment.

To make space for new code, **replace** all of the code inside `withTaskGroup(...)`'s closure with:

```
let batchSize = 4

for index in 0..<batchSize {
  group.addTask {
    await self.worker(number: index)
  }
}
```

Here, you define a batch size of four tasks to run concurrently, then start exactly four of them in your group. You still have sixteen more to run to complete the work. You'll cover those by adding a new task to the group **each time** a previous task completes. Insert this directly below the last code:

```
// 1
var index = batchSize

// 2
for await result in group {
  print("Completed: \(result)")
  // 3
  if index < total {
    group.addTask { [index] in
      await self.worker(number: index)
    }
    index += 1
  }
}
```

In this code, you:

1. Define a starting index and set it to the batch size.

2. Loop over any completing tasks and print "Completed …".

3. Then, as long as the current index is less than the total number of tasks, you add one more task to the group.

This is a fine example of how flexible the task group APIs are in reality. Namely:

• You iterate over the results **and** add fresh tasks at the same time.

• You control **how many** tasks can run at the same time.

• Last but not least, you don't need to change anything outside withTaskGroup(...) because these logic changes are **completely transparent** to the consumer.

Adding tasks to a group while it's running allows you to do many interesting things, including (but not limited) to:

• Keeping a group running indefinitely by always adding more and more tasks.

• Retrying tasks by re-adding them to the group upon failure.

• Inserting a high-priority UI task after either a set number of computational tasks finish running or you find a given result.

With these fresh ideas in mind, build and run. Tap **Engage systems**.

This time, the scan indicators paint a different picture:

You continuously remain at four scheduled tasks because, as soon as one completes, you schedule a new one in its place.

The second indicator, however, shows that you advance the total amount of work by only two (or however many you saw before) tasks per second. That matches what you established earlier in the chapter — namely, that the Swift runtime "gives" your group a device-specific number of threads to run concurrent tasks on.

Congratulations, your new concurrent code works exactly as expected!

Running Code After All Tasks Have Completed

Oftentimes you'd like to do some cleanup, update the UI or do something else after you run a group. In your current project, you'd like to reset some indicators to not confuse the user when the scan is over.

You could always use `TaskGroup.waitForAll()` to wait on all the tasks, then add the cleanup code.

But in your current `runAllTasks()` implementation, you already wait for all the tasks to complete. As mentioned, the `for await` loop will only end when the group runs out of tasks.

So all you need to do is to add this code directly after the last loop in
`runAllTasks()`:

```
await MainActor.run {
    completed = 0
    countPerSecond = 0
    scheduled = 0
}
```

This sets the three indicators in the UI to zero at the end of the scan.

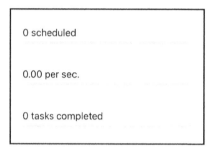

Easy! Now on to a more painful topic: error handling.

Group Error Handling

So far, running scans has been a walk in the park. `ScanTask` never fails and always
completes its heavy-duty work on time.

That will change in this section! `ScanTask.run()` will fail now and then, and you'll
have to cope with the consequences.

Open **ScanTask.swift** and scroll to `run()`. First, make the method throwing by
adding the `throws` keyword to its definition:

```
func run() async throws -> String {
```

Thrown errors move upward toward the calling code. You'll need to track that path
back to fix the compiler errors, which will help you visualize where the errors go.
Before you leave, though, add this line at the top of the method:

```
try await UnreliableAPI.shared.action(failingEvery: 10)
```

The starter project includes `UnreliableAPI`, which simply throws an error every few
calls so you can test some error handling scenarios.

Now that you're producing errors, you need to handle them. The code that calls run() now fails to compile because it's not using the try keyword.

Open **ScanModel.swift** and fix the compiler error in worker(number:) by adding try:

```
let result = try await task.run()
```

The next step is to modify the declaration of worker(number:) to also include throws:

```
func worker(number: Int) async throws -> String {
```

Then, scroll to runAllTasks() and add try to the two calls to worker(number:):

```
try await self.worker(number: index)
```

You now have throwing tasks, so you have to update the task group to also be a throwing one. Update the group creation call with the throwing variant withThrowingTaskGroup like so:

```
try await withThrowingTaskGroup(of: String.self) { [unowned
self] group in
```

Finally, group is now a ThrowingTaskGroup, so you must also update the for await loop :

```
for try await result in group {
```

The project now compiles once more. Build and run. Tap **Engage systems** and observe the app. Right around the time you see the completed task indicator go up to ten, the execution stops:

You don't catch errors anywhere in your model, so the error bubbles up and out of the group. The starter code in **SkyApp.swift** catches the error and presents it on-screen.

The result of this behavior is that, when one of your tasks throws, it "breaks" the whole group. Not only do further tasks not execute, you also don't get the results of the ones that have already completed.

In the next section, you'll redesign your code to ignore failing tasks and to collect the results of all the tasks that successfully return.

Using the Result Type With TaskGroup

To handle errors safely, you won't throw an error; instead, you'll use the `Result` type. If you haven't used `Result` before, it's a simple Swift enum with the following two cases:

- **success(Value)**: With an associated result.

- **failure(Error)**: With an associated error.

Open **ScanModel.swift** and scroll to `worker(number:)`. Then, change the method definition to avoid throwing errors and return a `Result` value instead. Update the complete function body to the following:

```
func worker(number: Int) async -> Result<String, Error> {
  await onScheduled()

  let task = ScanTask(input: number)

  let result: Result<String, Error>
  do {
    result = try .success(await task.run())
  } catch {
    result = .failure(error)
  }

  await onTaskCompleted()
  return result
}
```

Little has changed in the behavior of the method. The new code tries to call `run()` just as you did before, but this time around, you catch any errors and safely return `failure` instead.

Changing the return type threw some other compiler errors, which you'll now fix.

In `runAllTasks()`, you need to change the group return type from `String` to `Result<String, Error>`. Make that change on the line of `withThrowingTaskGroup(of: String.self)` so it looks like this:

```
withThrowingTaskGroup(of: Result<String, Error>.self)
```

That changes the group to expect a `Result` from each task; it also clears the compile errors. However, some warnings are still left, so you need to change the two occurrences of `try await self.worker(number: index)` back to:

```
await self.worker(number: index)
```

Sweet! Build and run. Tap **Engage systems**. Now, the app works through all the tasks, skipping over any that fail.

Note how the alert box says you worked through 20 scan tasks, but the lowest indicator shows that 18 tasks actually finished. The difference between the two results is the number of tasks that failed.

Now, you only need to take care of the logs. Right now, you print the raw `Result` description, which is a bit untidy:

```
Completed: success("5")
Completed: success("7")
Completed: success("6")
Completed: failure(Sky.UnreliableAPI.Error())
Completed: success("8")
Completed: success("10")
```

Scroll to `print("Completed: \(result)")` and replace it with:

```
switch result {
case .success(let result):
  print("Completed: \(result)")
case .failure(let error):
  print("Failed: \(error.localizedDescription)")
}
```

Build and run. Scan again, and you will have a nicer looking log:

```
Completed: 5
Completed: 6
Completed: 7
Failed: UnreliableAPI.action(failingEvery:) failed.
Completed: 10
Completed: 8
Completed: 12
```

And that's a wrap! You've now learned a ton about using `TaskGroup` and its flexibility and power.

But your search for alien life isn't over! In Chapter 10, "Actors in a Distributed System", you'll increase your scanning power by working on a new version of Sky called **SkyNet** that is able to take over other devices on the network and use their resources to perform even more scans in parallel. I'm sure "you'll be back" to read that one!

Key Points

- To run an arbitrary number of concurrent tasks, create a **task group**. Do this by using the function `withTaskGroup(of:returning:body:)`. For a throwing task group, use `withThrowingTaskGroup(of:returning:body:)`.

- You can **add tasks** to a group by calling `addTask(priority:operation:)` or `addTaskUnlessCancelled(priority:operation:)`.

- Control task execution by **canceling the group** via `cancelAll()` or **waiting for all tasks to complete** with `waitForAll()`.

- Use the group as an **asynchronous sequence** to iterate over each task result in real time.

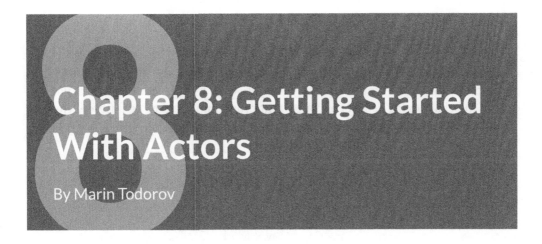

Chapter 8: Getting Started With Actors

By Marin Todorov

In the last chapter, you used the `TaskGroup` and `ThrowingTaskGroup` APIs to execute tasks in parallel. This lets you do work faster should a single CPU core not suffice your needs.

You explored `TaskGroup`'s ingenious design, which allows you to run tasks **in parallel** but still collect the execution's results in a safe, **serial** manner by iterating the group as an asynchronous sequence.

execution

As mentioned in the "Mutating Shared State" subsection of the previous chapter, some problems require you to update your state from a concurrent context. That's one of the challenging aspects of concurrent programming: taming different threads that try to access the same piece of memory at the same time.

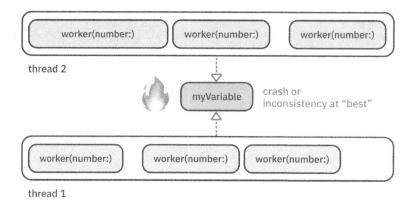

This chapter will cover how the new Swift concurrency model addresses data races by using a new type: **actor**.

Before you dive into this new type, you'll take a moment to understand what the issue with updating mutable state *really* is.

Understanding Thread-safe Code

You might have seen methods described as **thread-safe** in documentation from Apple or third-party frameworks.

This usually means that, regardless of whether you're calling an API from the main thread or a so-called background thread, the method will always behave as expected. In other words, the method will still work, even when multiple threads call it at the same time.

> **Note**: The concept of thread-safe code is also sometimes referred to as *linearizability* or *atomicity*, which aims to limit the outcomes of concurrently accessing an object from multiple processes.

Unfortunately, in Objective-C and versions of Swift before 5.5, there was no syntax to mark a method as thread-safe. You had to rely on each method's documentation to find out whether it was safe or not.

Third-party frameworks sometimes give you access to their source, but that doesn't always solve the problem. For example, can you tell immediately if this piece of code is thread-safe?

```
class Counter {
  private var count = 0

  func increment() {
    count += 1
  }
}
```

As you see, nothing stands out when you look at Counter that would make it particularly *unsafe*.

And yet, if two threads running in parallel both call Counter.increment(), you could end up increasing count by either one or two — the exact outcome being *unpredictable*. Even worse, if the two calls to Counter.increment() happen at *precisely* the same moment — your app will crash.

Even more worrisome is that crashes rarely happen when you compile your app for debugging — for example, when the app is running in your iOS simulator or you started it from Xcode on your device. Release builds are the ones that are optimized and fast enough to produce a data-race crash.

Therefore, you can say that *any code* that doesn't take proactive steps towards protecting shared mutable state from concurrent access is inherently **not thread-safe**.

Traditionally developers used **locks, semaphores** or **serial dispatch queues** to ensure exclusive access to shared state. With a lock, for example, a thread locks the access to a shared resource, and other threads need to wait for it to unlock before they can read or write to that same resource.

Effectively, threads lock each other out to guarantee exclusive access to the resource:

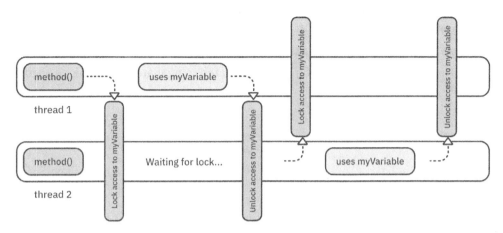

Concurrent code that uses lock APIs — like `OSAllocatedUnfairLock` — is fairly fast and safe when written well. The previous code sample looks like this when you use a lock:

```swift
class Counter {
  private var lock = OSAllocatedUnfairLock()
  private var count = 0

  func increment() {
    lock.withLock {
      count += 1
    }
  }
}
```

The code does actually look pretty straightforward — every code that's wrapped in a `withLock {...}` runs exclusively to any other code that uses the same lock.

However, do you remember why you looked into this section's code sample in the first place? As a developer using this API, how can you tell if calling `Counter.increment()` is thread-safe or not? Furthermore, how can the compiler itself know your code is thread-safe, so it can help protect you from any races resulting from a developer mistake, for example?

If you don't have access to the code, or the free time to read it thoroughly, there's really no way to tell if it's really safe. That's where actors come in.

Meeting Actor

The **actor type** is one of the concurrency-related improvements introduced in Swift 5.5. actor is a programming type just like its peers: enum, struct, class and so on. More specifically, it's a reference type like class.

The code looks quite familiar, too. Here's the example from the previous section. This time, however, it replaces the keyword class with actor to make it thread-safe:

```
actor Counter {
  private var count = 0

  func increment() {
    count += 1
  }
}
```

Unlike with the class-based variant, this type guarantees that no more than one execution of increment() runs at a time and therefore an always-exclusive mutation of count.

Actors are an existing, well-established **model for concurrent computation**. You can read about them in detail in Wikipedia's Actor model (https://en.wikipedia.org/wiki/Actor_model) article.

Actors behave according to a few basic rules that allow them to guarantee the safety of their internal state. Different implementations vary across languages, so in this chapter, you'll learn how actors function *specifically* in Swift.

An actor in Swift can safely access and mutate its own state. A special type called a **serial executor**, which the runtime manages, synchronizes all calls to the actor's members. The serial executor, much like a serial dispatch queue in GCD, executes tasks one after another. By doing this, it protects the actor's state from concurrent access:

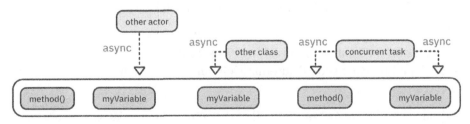

actor serial executor

When you look up the `Actor` protocol (https://developer.apple.com/documentation/swift/actor), which all actors adhere to, you'll see there's only a single requirement. Namely, all actors must have a property called `unownedExecutor`, which is the aforementioned executor that serializes access to the actor state.

But what about the real cause of data races? How can you guarantee another type won't call your actor from multiple threads at the same time and cause a crash?

`actor` has a special deal with the Swift compiler to take care of that.

Access to the actor from other types is automatically performed asynchronously and scheduled on the actor's serial executor. This is called the **state isolation layer**, outlined here:

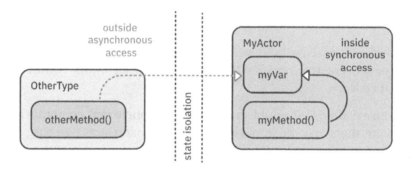

The state isolation layer ensures that all state mutation is **thread-safe**. `actor` itself is the guarantee of thread-safety for consumers of the API, the compiler and the runtime.

Recognizing the Main Actor

You've already worked with actors in this book, although they were only mentioned in passing. Any time you had to work on UI-related code, you ran it on the **main actor**.

You ran code on the main actor by calling `MainActor.run(...)`. Additionally, you annotated methods that should automatically run on the main actor with `@MainActor`.

Is the main actor an `actor` type with all of the actor behaviors discussed above?

Yes, indeed! The main actor runs code serially on the main thread and protects its shared state: the UI of your app. It's a **global actor** that's accessible from anywhere, and you can use its **shared instance** across your app.

You'll learn more about global actors in Chapter 9, "Global Actors".

Next, it's time to get started with this chapter's project — implementing your first `actor` types.

Getting Started with Actors

EmojiArt is an app that lets you browse an online catalog of digital emoji art. To verify that the digital art is authentic, the app reads the feed of current works of art from the server, verifies the digital signature of the images and, only then, displays them onscreen.

Open the starter version of EmojiArt in this chapter's materials, under **projects/ starter**.

Like all projects in this book, EmojiArt's SwiftUI views, navigation and data models are already wired up and ready to go. This app has more code than this book's other projects, but you'll use it to work through a lot of concepts throughout this and the next chapters.

> **Note**: Like the rest of this book's projects, EmojiArt uses sample data to teach a set of concepts; it's not an actual digital art store.

You use an actor when you want to protect a state from concurrent mutation. You'll try out actors for the first time by implementing the app's loading screen.

You'll display a live-updating progress bar of the feed's verification process and use an actor to safely update the progress value from concurrently running tasks.

Before getting started with the project, start the book server. If you haven't already done that, navigate to the server folder **00-book-server** in the book materials-repository and enter `swift run`. The detailed steps are covered in Chapter 1, "Why Modern Swift Concurrency?".

Now, build and run the project. Take a look at EmojiArt's initial state:

Here, you see `LoadingView`, which will run the verification onscreen. Once that's done, the app will navigate to `ListView`, which displays the actual art pieces.

You haven't implemented the model method that verifies the images yet, so the progress bar is stuck at zero percent with no chance of completion. You'll fix that as you work through this chapter.

Mutating State Concurrently

Open the app's model file, **EmojiArtModel.swift**, and add this new code inside the class:

> **Note**: If you already ran the app, you'll see a warning about updating the UI from a background thread. Ignore it for now; you'll fix it shortly.

```
private(set) var verifiedCount = 0

func verifyImages() async throws {
  try await withThrowingTaskGroup(of: Void.self) { group in

  }
}
```

`verifiedCount` is the verification counter that you'll update concurrently. `verifyImages()` is the method that will verify the individual pieces of artwork. To perform concurrent work, you create a new task group via `withThrowingTaskGroup(...)`, as you did in the previous chapter.

Unlike before, however, you'll update your state *directly* from the task body so that mutation happens **concurrently** and in **real time**.

To perform the verification, insert the following code inside `withThrowingTaskGroup(...)`'s trailing closure:

```
imageFeed.forEach { file in
  group.addTask { [unowned self] in
    try await Checksum.verify(file.checksum)
    self.verifiedCount += 1
  }
}

try await group.waitForAll()
```

In the code above, you iterate over the image files in `imageFeed`, assuming the model has already fetched those from the server, and add a new task for each file. If `Checksum.verify(_:)` detects an asset with an invalid checksum, it throws an error. Otherwise, the asset is valid and you increase `verifiedCount` by one.

Finally, you use `group.waitForAll()` to wait for all tasks to complete and re-throw any task errors out of the group.

> **Note**: As you know, the group implicitly waits for its tasks to complete before returning. However, if you don't use any `try` keywords inside the group closure, the compiler decides you want a non-throwing group and will not re-throw task errors! To fix this, you use `waitForAll()` prefixed with `try` to hint to the compiler that it should use a throwing group after all.

Given all your experience with these book's projects, you're likely already rolling your eyes because you know that mutating `verifiedCount` from within the task is unsafe. No worries, you'll fix that in a moment.

Showing the Art and Updating the Progress

You'll start by adding a call to `verifyImages(...)` in the screen showing the verification indicator. Open **LoadingView.swift** and scroll to the `task { ... }` view modifier.

Just below `try await model.loadImages()` — the line that fetches the image feed from the server — insert:

```
try await model.verifyImages()
withAnimation {
  isVerified = true
}
```

After successfully fetching the feed, you call `verifyImages()` to verify the authenticity of the assets. Finally, you set `isVerified` to `true`. Changing `isVerified` causes the main view to replace `LoadingView` with `ListView` and display the image feed onscreen.

Build and run. You'll see that, shortly after displaying LoadingView, the image feed pops up. The thumbnails aren't visible right now, but you can see the names and prices of the works of art.

Since you update verifiedCount concurrently and want to avoid overwhelming the main thread, you'll add a timer to LoadingView that will periodically update the progress bar during verification.

Add this new view modifier to LoadingView, just below where the alert modifier code wraps up:

```
.onReceive(timer) { _ in
  guard !model.imageFeed.isEmpty else { return }

  progress = Double(model.verifiedCount) /
Double(model.imageFeed.count)
}
```

The starter code for LoadingView includes a ready-to-go timer property called timer. In onReceive(_:perform:), you subscribe to this timer and make sure there are actually feed items, to avoid unnecessary updates.

Finally, you divide the number of verified assets by the count of all images, then update progress. This will update the progress bar with the latest value a few times per second.

Build and run one more time. You'll now see the verification go through to one hundred percent.

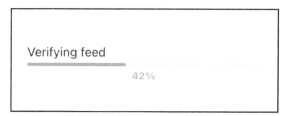

Surprisingly, everything seems to be running just fine with *no crashes*, despite the concurrent updates.

So *are there* any race conditions in the code you just wrote? It's quite hard to tell, considering the app is compiled for debugging and doesn't have any optimizations. This might mean the app is just *too slow* to reproduce this scenario, compared to an optimized release version that is more prone to triggering a data race.

Detecting Race Conditions

One way to detect data races in your code is to enable the **Thread Sanitizer** in your Xcode project scheme. Click the scheme selector in Xcode's toolbar and select **Edit scheme…**:

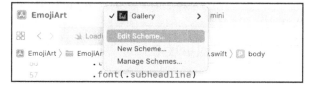

Next, in the scheme window, click **Run**, then select the **Diagnostics** tab. Check the **Thread Sanitizer** checkbox and, finally, close the scheme editing window.

When you rebuild the project, Xcode will bake some extra checks into your app. At runtime, these will verify whether your code concurrently mutates any data.

Build and run. Let the app load and switch to the feed screen.

The app UI looks the same as before. If you direct your attention to Xcode, however, you'll notice a new purple runtime warning. Unfold the warning details in the Debug navigator in the left-hand sidebar and you will see all the places in the project that tried to access or mutate some shared state causing a data race:

```
71    private(set) var verifiedCount = 0
72
73    func verifyImages() async throws {
74        try await withThrowingTaskGroup(of: Void.self) { group
75            imageFeed.forEach { file in
76                group.addTask { [unowned self] in
77                    try await Checksum.verify(file.checksum)
78                    self.verifiedCount += 1   ⌫ Write of size 8 by thre...
79                }
80            }
81
82            try await group.waitForAll()
83        }
84    }
85 }
```

If Thread Sanitizers detects a data race, the code will eventually crash in production. This is *no bueno*.

Using Actors to Protect Shared Mutable State

To protect `EmojiArtModel.verifiedCount` from concurrent access, you'll convert `EmojiArtModel` from a class to an actor. Since actors exhibit a lot of typical class behavior, such as by-reference semantics, the change shouldn't be too complex.

Open **EmojiArtModel.swift** and replace `class EmojiArtModel: ObservableObject` with:

```
actor EmojiArtModel: ObservableObject
```

This changes the type of the model to an actor. Your shared state is now safe!

As you see in Xcode, actors don't magically solve concurrent access — you're now facing a compile error. The compiler now follows the rules for actors and finds issues in the code that used to compile before.

In other words, some of your code that used to work **doesn't compile** as an actor. The compiler doesn't magically solve the issues; instead, it **suggests how you should change** your code to make it work safely in a concurrent context. But more importantly, when you use an actor, the compiler **protects** you against creating unsafe thread accesses in your code.

Now, you'll follow Xcode's directions to make the existing code thread-safe.

The error says:

```
"Actor-isolated property 'verifiedCount' can not be mutated from
a Sendable closure".
```

You'll learn about `Sendable` in the next sections. For now, just know you get the error because you can't update the actor state from "outside" of its direct scope.

This chapter's introduction mentioned that all code that **isn't confined to the serial executor** of the actor is "outside" access. That means it includes calls from other types and concurrent tasks — like your `TaskGroup`, in this case.

To overcome this issue, you'll extract the code to increment `verifiedCount` into a method, then call it asynchronously. This allows the actor to serialize the calls to that method.

Add this new method anywhere inside `EmojiArtModel`:

```
private func increaseVerifiedCount() {
  verifiedCount += 1
}
```

As discussed before, you can call this method synchronously from "inside" the actor's direct scope, but the compiler will **enforce asynchronous access** from "outside" of it.

Now, find `self.verifiedCount += 1` in your concurrent task code. Replace it with:

```
await self.increaseVerifiedCount()
```

This new code will make calls to `increaseVerifiedCount()` serially; this ensures you mutate your shared state safely.

Sadly, once you resolve that error, you still face a whole bunch of compiler errors. Now that `imageFeed` is part of your `EmojiArtModel` actor, you can't access that property on the main actor. *Oh, the terror!* SwiftUI runs on the main actor and can't read the feed anymore. You'll fix that next.

Sharing Data Across Actors

Given that you mostly use `EmojiArtModel.imageFeed` to drive the app's UI, it makes sense to place this property on the main actor. But how can you **share** it between the main actor and `EmojiArtModel`?

In this section, you'll move `imageFeed` to execute on the main actor, but the property itself will remain inside `EmojiArtModel`. It sounds a bit *esoteric*, but it's actually straightforward. In fact, **you've already done it** many times in this book — by using the `@MainActor` attribute.

Open **EmojiArtModel.swift** and scroll to `imageFeed`. Annotate the property with `@MainActor`, so it looks like this:

```
@Published @MainActor private(set) var imageFeed: [ImageFile] =
[]
```

This code moves `imageFeed` from the `EmojiArtModel`'s serial executor to the main actor. That clears the compile errors in the SwiftUI code because `imageFeed` is now accessible from the main thread.

To fix the rest of the errors, replace `imageFeed.removeAll()` in `loadImages()` with:

```
await MainActor.run {
   imageFeed.removeAll()
}
```

And replace `imageFeed = list` with:

```
await MainActor.run {
   imageFeed = list
}
```

The new code makes a little detour from running code on your actor's executor. Instead, it runs the two calls asynchronously on the main actor, where it's safe to update the UI:

You've now fixed almost all the errors; you'll take care of the rest next.

> **Note**: If you're using Xcode 14 some of these errors might not disappear voluntarily. If you feel that you've fixed a code issue but a related error is still showing up, click Product/Clear All Issues in Xcode's main menu to reset the displayed diagnostics.

Fixing the Remaining Errors

Scroll to `verifyImages()` and find the error on the line that calls `imageFeed.forEach { ... }`. To access the actor, you need to call `imageFeed.forEach { ... }` asynchronously.

Prepend an `await` before the call, like this:

```
await imageFeed.forEach { file in
```

There's one final error left in **LoadingView.swift**. Toward the bottom of the file, there's an error on the line that calculates the value of `progress`:

```
Actor-isolated property 'verifiedCount' can not be referenced
from the main actor
```

Prepend the math expression with an `await` and wrap the offending line in a `Task`, like so:

```
Task {
  progress = await Double(model.verifiedCount) /
    Double(model.imageFeed.count)
}
```

Congratulations, you've followed Xcode's guidance to completion and fixed all the unsafe code. Build and run again. This time, there aren't any purple warnings!

At this point in the chapter, you've worked through designing your first actor type and experienced some actor-specific compiler behavior. But there's one topic you skipped over: What is the `Sendable` type that those compiler errors mentioned? You'll learn about `Sendable` next.

Understanding Sendable

`Sendable` is a protocol that indicates that a given value is **safe to use in concurrent code**. "Use how?" you might ask. Dig in and see.

Open the `Sendable` protocol's documentation page (https://developer.apple.com/documentation/swift/sendable).

Scroll down a bit to the **Inherited By** section, and you'll see that a few protocols inherit from `Sendable`. For example, the `Actor` protocol is a `Sendable`; therefore, actor instances are safe to use in concurrent code. That makes sense.

In the next section, **Conforming Types**, you'll see that many types in Swift are sendable by default; for example: `Bool`, `Double`, `Int`, `StaticString`, `UnsafePointer` and others are all safe to use in concurrent code.

Generally speaking, value types are safe to use in concurrent code because value semantics prevent you from accidentally mutating a shared reference to the same object.

Classes are generally not sendable because their by-reference semantics allow you to **mutate the same instance in memory**. You did so earlier in this chapter, when you mutated `verifiedCount` on the same model instance concurrently.

You use the `@Sendable` attribute to **require thread-safe values** in your code. In other words, you use it to require that values must conform to the `Sendable` protocol.

For example, look at the `Task` type. Because it creates an asynchronous task that could unsafely mutate shared state, the `Task.init(...)` declaration **requires** that the `operation` closure is `Sendable`:

```
init(
  priority: TaskPriority? = nil,
  operation: @escaping @Sendable () async -> Success
)
```

The `operation` closure is `@escaping` because it's asynchronous and also `@Sendable`, which **verifies at compile-time** that the closure code is thread-safe. You already experienced this protection first-hand when you got compiler errors for trying to mutate shared state from inside `TaskGroup.addTask(...)`.

To fully understand the role of the `Sendable` protocol, take a moment to have another look at its documentation page (https://developer.apple.com/documentation/swift/sendable). Note how this protocol has *no requirements* — you really only use it to annotate types that you know are safe to use across threads.

Once you add `Sendable` conformance to one of your types, the compiler will automatically limit it in various ways to help you ensure its thread safety. For example, it'll ask you to make classes final, class properties immutable, and so on.

Look up `addTask(...)` and you'll see it also requires a `Sendable` closure:

```
mutating func addTask(
  priority: TaskPriority? = nil,
  operation: @escaping @Sendable () async -> ChildTaskResult
)
```

Therefore, the best practice in your own code is to require that any closures you run asynchronously be `@Sendable`, and that any values you use in asynchronous code adhere to the `Sendable` protocol.

Additionally, if your struct or class is thread-safe, you should also add `Sendable` conformance so other concurrent code can use it safely.

Making Safe Methods nonisolated

Now that you've moved `imageFeed` off your own actor and onto the main actor, the methods that work with the feed don't actually work with your actor's shared state *directly*.

Back in **EmojiArtModel.swift**, scroll to `loadImages()` and check the code. None of it reads from or mutates either `imageFeed` or `verifiedCount`. You update `imageFeed` from the main actor, then the main actor serializes execution by default.

So in fact, `loadImages()` and `downloadImage(_:)` don't have *any state* to protect anymore. Therefore, they don't need the actor behavior at all.

When methods like that are safe, you can aid the runtime and remove the safety harness around them by marking them with the `nonisolated` keyword.

Prepend the `loadImages()` declaration with `nonisolated` like so:

```
nonisolated func loadImages() async throws
```

Next, do the same for `downloadImage(_:)`:

```
nonisolated func downloadImage(_ image: ImageFile) async throws
  -> Data
```

With these changes, the two methods behave as if they are vanilla **class** methods instead of **actor** methods. You also get a small performance win from removing the safety checks. You probably won't feel it if you call these methods a few times, but in a highly concurrent context, you'll see some speed improvement.

Designing More Complex Actors

Now that you've created a fairly simple actor, it's time to try a more complex design. You'll mix actors, tasks and `async/await` to solve one of the eternal problems in programming: **image caching**.

Throughout the rest of the chapter, you'll build an actor that fetches the digital emoji assets from the book server and caches them in memory.

To start, add a new file to the project and call it **ImageLoader.swift**. Replace the placeholder code with the bare bones of that new actor:

```swift
import UIKit

actor ImageLoader {
  enum DownloadState {
    case inProgress(Task<UIImage, Error>)
    case completed(UIImage)
    case failed
  }

  private(set) var cache: [String: DownloadState] = [:]
}
```

In essence, this actor manages a cache dictionary that will store both the ongoing downloads and the images you've downloaded already.

cache contains values of type DownloadState, which can have one of these three download states:

- **inProgress**: The asset download has started but hasn't finished yet. This case gives you the **in-flight task**, which lets you await its completion and get the resulting image directly.

- **completed**: You've already downloaded the asset, and you're keeping the UIImage in memory.

- **failed**: You already tried downloading the asset with the given path, but the server returned an error.

Filling up the Cache

Next, you'll add a few methods to manage the cache: adding images, starting a new download and clearing the cache.

First, you'll use a method to add an image asset to the in-memory cache. Add this next method to your new actor:

```swift
func add(_ image: UIImage, forKey key: String) {
  cache[key] = .completed(image)
}
```

You can directly mutate cache from actor methods, so you simply set the value for the given asset key to .completed(image).

Next, you'll add a method to fetch a single image. It will get the image from memory if you've downloaded it already. Otherwise, it will get the image from the server. Start by checking the in-memory cache:

```
func image(_ serverPath: String) async throws -> UIImage {
  if let cached = cache[serverPath] {
    switch cached {
    case .completed(let image):
      return image
    case .inProgress(let task):
      return try await task.value
    case .failed: throw "Download failed"
    }
  }
}
```

If you find a value matching the asset key in cache, you use one of these three options:

- If the asset has finished downloading, you return the associated image.

- If the asset download is in progress, you await the associated task and return its value. This way, the original request will run as normal. The runtime will suspend here and return once the task completes.

- Finally, if the asset fails to download, you simply throw an error.

Next, it's time to add some code to download an image from the server if you don't find the asset in the local cache. Append the following code to the bottom of image(_:):

```
let download: Task<UIImage, Error> = Task.detached {
  guard let url = URL(string: "http://
localhost:8080".appending(serverPath))
  else {
    throw "Could not create the download URL"
  }
  print("Download: \(url.absoluteString)")
  let data = try await URLSession.shared.data(from: url).0
  return try resize(data, to: CGSize(width: 200, height: 200))
}

cache[serverPath] = .inProgress(download)
```

Similar to previous chapters, you create a detached asynchronous task and download the image from the server. To keep track of the ongoing downloads, you print a debug log to the console.

Before returning, you call the starter-project function `resize(_:to:)` to scale down the server image and store it as a thumbnail.

Finally, once the task is ready, you add it to `cache` as an `inProgress` value. Should the same asset pop up in the feed again, you won't download it a second time. Instead, you'll wait for the ongoing `download` task to complete and return the fetched result.

Wrapping up the Image Download

Last but not least, you need to handle the result of the download. Append this last piece of code to `image(_:)`:

```
do {
  let result = try await download.value
  add(result, forKey: serverPath)
  return result
} catch {
  cache[serverPath] = .failed
  throw error
}
```

Here, you wait for the download task to complete, then you call `add(_:forKey:)` to add the image to the in-memory cache and return it.

If the task throws, you update `cache` with a `failure` value for this asset before re-throwing the error.

With that, you've finished the actor's main logic. Before moving on, add one last convenience method to the actor:

```
func clear() {
  cache.removeAll()
}
```

You'll use `clear()` in the next chapter to clear the in-memory cache for debugging purposes.

Having finalized the new actor, you need to "spread the love" around your app so all the views can use it to display images.

Sharing the Actor

Since you'll use `ImageLoader` in a few different views, your next step is to inject it directly into the SwiftUI environment, so you can easily access it throughout your view hierarchy.

To use it as an environment object, though, you need to adhere to `ObservableObject`. Your loader doesn't feature any published properties, but SwiftUI requires an `ObservableObject` conformance anyway.

Open **ImageLoader.swift** and, at the top, add an `ObservableObject` conformance, like so:

```
actor ImageLoader: ObservableObject
```

Luckily, unlike other directions in this chapter, this change causes no compile errors. You can just move on with the next steps.

Open **AppMain.swift** and, under `ListView()`, add this modifier to inject the loader to the view hierarchy:

```
.environmentObject(ImageLoader())
```

Now, you can use `ImageLoader` from any view where you need images.

Another view bundled with the starter code, `ThumbImage`, displays a single asset in the image feed, so this is certainly a place where you'll need `ImageLoader`. Open **ThumbImage.swift** and add this new property to the type:

```
@EnvironmentObject var imageLoader: ImageLoader
```

This line initializes the injected image loader. You'll use it to fetch the asset image.

Move on to `ThumbImage`'s view body, where you'll add one more modifier to start the thumbnail download. Directly after `overlay(...)`, add:

```
.task {
  guard let image = try? await imageLoader.image(file.url) else
{
    overlay = "camera.metering.unknown"
    return
  }
  updateImage(image)
}
```

When the thumbnail view appears onscreen, you call `imageLoader.image(_:)` to fetch the image from the server. If the image has already been downloaded, you return the cached image instead. If the download fails, you set an overlay for the thumbnail to show the user that the image load failed.

Finally, if everything was a success, you update the view image by calling `updateImage(_:)`.

Build and run. *At last*, you can enjoy some cool emoji art.

Wow, those "art" pieces aren't cheap!

> **Note**: If you want to "save" a few hundred dollars for an emoji art piece, you can peek into the book server's code and see how to draw a gradient in Swift and add an emoji on top. Anyone can be an "artist"!

Using the Cached Assets

The server image feed intentionally returns some duplicate assets so you can play around with the scenario of getting an already-cached asset and displaying it.

When you look at Xcode's output console, you'll initially see some download logs like these:

```
Download: http://localhost:8080/gallery/image?11
Download: http://localhost:8080/gallery/image?16
Download: http://localhost:8080/gallery/image?23
Download: http://localhost:8080/gallery/image?26
```

Scroll all the way to the bottom of the feed, and you'll see that the download logs stop appearing in the console, even if you keep scrolling up and down. Once you've downloaded all the assets, you only fetch images from memory!

To wrap this section up, open **DetailsView.swift**, where you'll add some code to display a larger version of a selected asset.

Add the same `imageLoader` environment object property:

```
@EnvironmentObject var imageLoader: ImageLoader
```

Add a `task` modifier just below the last `foregroundColor` modifier towards the bottom of the file with the following code:

```
.task {
  image = try? await imageLoader.image(file.url)
}
```

Build and run. Tap an image and enjoy the details preview:

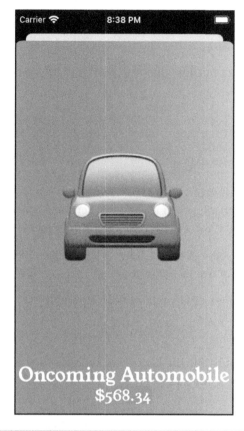

> **Note**: The details view shows the given unicode name for each emoji. Some of those names are pretty weird — I'm looking at you, "White Smiling Facevariation Selector16"!

Congratulations, the EmojiArt online catalog app is complete. Well, at least the part you had to work on in this chapter. You'll explore some more opportunities to use actors in the next chapter.

Key Points

- The **actor** type is a type that protects its internals from concurrent access, supported by compile-time checks and diagnostics.

- Actors allow **"internal" synchronous access** to their state while the compiler enforces **asynchronous calls for access** from the "outside".

- Actor methods prefixed with the **nonisolated** keyword behave as standard class methods and provide no isolation mechanics.

- Actors use a runtime-managed **serial executor** to serialize calls to methods and access to properties.

- The **Sendable** protocol indicates a value is safe to use in a concurrent context. The **@Sendable** attribute requires a sendable value for a method or a closure parameter.

In this hands-on chapter, you designed both simple and complex actor-based code. Most importantly, you experienced some of the hurdles of converting unsafe class code to thread-safe actor code.

The fun isn't over yet, though. You'll keep working on the EmojiArt app as you learn about **global actors** in the next chapter.

For the grand finale, you'll once again search for alien life in Chapter 10, "Actors in a Distributed System", where you'll learn about using actors that work together across different devices.

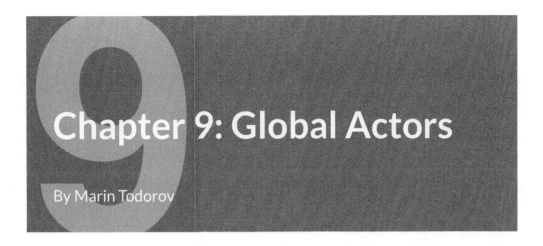

Chapter 9: Global Actors

By Marin Todorov

In the previous chapter, you got to meet Swift's `actor` type, which provides code with safe, concurrent access to its internal state. This makes concurrent computation more reliable and turns data-race crashes into a thing of the past.

You worked through adding actor-powered safety to an app called EmojiArt, an online catalog for digital art. Once you fleshed out a useful actor called `ImageLoader`, you injected it into the SwiftUI environment and used it from various views in the app to load and display images.

Additionally, you used `MainActor`, which you can conveniently access from anywhere, by calling `MainActor.run(...)`. That's pretty handy given how often you need to make quick changes that drive the UI:

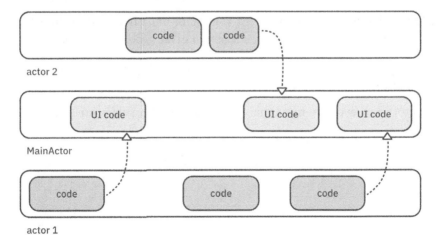

When you think about it, this is super-duper convenient: Because your app runs on a **single main thread**, you can't create a second or a third MainActor. So *it does* make sense that there's a default, shared instance of that actor that you can safely use from anywhere.

Some examples of app-wide, single-instance shared state are:

- The app's database layer, which is usually a singleton type that manages the state of a file on disk.

- Image or data caches are also often single-instance types.

- The authentication status of the user is valid app-wide, whether they have logged in or not.

Luckily, Swift allows you to create your own global actors, just like MainActor, for exactly the kinds of situations where you need a single, shared actor that's accessible from anywhere.

Getting to Meet GlobalActor

In Swift, you can annotate an actor with the @globalActor attribute, which makes it automatically conform to the GlobalActor protocol:

```
@globalActor actor MyActor {
  ...
}
```

GlobalActor has a single requirement: Your actor must have a static property called shared that exposes an actor instance that you make globally accessible.

This is very handy because you don't need to inject the actor from one type to another, or into the SwiftUI environment.

Global actors, however, are more than just a stand-in for singleton types.

Just as you annotated methods with @MainActor to allow their code to change the app's UI, you can use the @-prefixed annotation to **automatically execute methods** on your own, custom global actor:

```
@MyActor func say(_ text: String) {
   ... automatically runs on MyActor ...
}
```

To automatically execute a method on your own global actor, annotate it with the name of your actor prefixed with an @ sign, like so: @MyActor, @DatabaseActor, @ImageLoader and so on.

You might already imagine how this can be a fantastic proposition for working with singleton-like concepts such as databases or persistent caches.

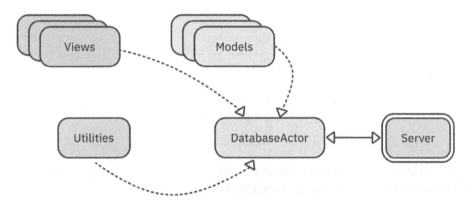

To avoid concurrency problems you need to annotate all the relevant methods and make them run on your global actor.

In fact, you can annotate a **complete class** with a global actor and that will add that actor's semantics to all its methods and properties (as long as they aren't nonisolated):

```
@MyActor class MyClass {
   ...
}
```

Lastly, by using the @ annotation, you can **group** methods or entire types that can safely share mutable state in their own **synchronized silo**:

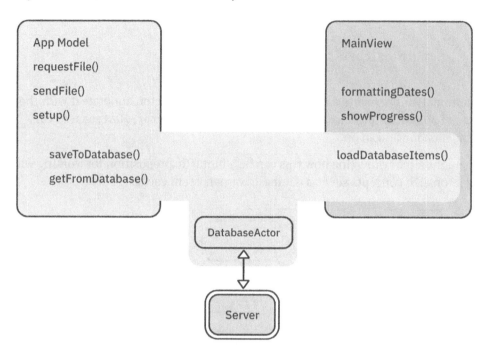

In this chapter, you'll add a persistent cache layer to the EmojiArt project that you worked on in the last chapter, as shown in the diagram above.

You'll get plenty of opportunities to learn about global actors in detail while having fun with juggling on-disk and in-memory caches.

Continuing With the EmojiArt Project

In this section, you'll keep working on the last chapter's project: **EmojiArt**, your online store for verified, digital emoji art:

In Chapter 8, "Getting Started With Actors", you implemented an actor-based, in-memory cache. Your ImageLoader actor manages a dictionary of completed downloads, failed downloads and those still being processed, so you don't fire duplicate requests to the server.

However, when you quit the app and run it again, it needs to fetch the images from the server all over again. They don't persist on the device.

This is a perfect opportunity for you to add a global actor to upgrade your app with a persistent, on-disk cache.

If you worked through the entirety of Chapter 8, "Getting Started With Actors", you can continue working on your own project. Otherwise, open the EmojiArt starter project in this chapter's materials from the **projects/starter** folder.

Before getting started with the project, start the book server. If you haven't already done that, navigate to the server folder **00-book-server** in the book materials-repository and enter `swift run`. The detailed steps are covered in Chapter 1, "Why Modern Swift Concurrency?".

At this point, you're all set to start working!

Creating a Global Actor

In this section, you'll enhance EmojiArt with a new global actor that will persist downloaded images on disk.

To start, create a new Swift file and name it **ImageDatabase.swift**. Replace the placeholder code with the actor's bare bones:

```swift
import UIKit

@globalActor actor ImageDatabase {
  static let shared = ImageDatabase()

}
```

Here, you declare a new actor called `ImageDatabase` and annotate it with `@globalActor`. This makes the type conform to the `GlobalActor` protocol, which you satisfy by adding the `shared` property right away.

In more complex use cases, the shared instance could also be an actor of a different type. In this chapter, you'll use `shared` simply to facilitate access to the default instance of `ImageDatabase`.

Now, you can access your new actor type from anywhere by referring to the shared instance `ImageDatabase.shared`. Additionally, you can move the execution methods of other types to the `ImageDatabase` serial executor by annotating them with `@ImageDatabase`.

> **Note:** The Actor and GlobalActor protocols don't require an initializer. If you'd like to create new instances of your global actor, however, you can add a public or internal initializer. This is a valid approach when, for example, you create a custom instance to use in your unit tests.
>
> On the other hand, if you want to explicitly avoid creating other copies, add an init() and make it private.

To wrap up the basic actor structure and its state, add these properties to it:

```
let imageLoader = ImageLoader()

private let storage = DiskStorage()
private var storedImagesIndex = Set<String>()
```

Now, your new actor will use an instance of ImageLoader to automatically fetch images that aren't already fetched from the server.

You also instantiate a class called DiskStorage, which handles the disk-access layer for you, so you don't have to write non-actor-related code. DiskStorage features simple file operation methods like reading, writing and deleting files from the app's caches.

Finally, you'll keep an index of the persisted files on disk in storedImagesIndex. This lets you avoid checking the file system every time you send a request to ImageDatabase.

Is it possible that you introduced some concurrency issues into your code with these few simple lines? You'll check that out next.

Creating a Safe Silo

Above, you introduced two dependencies to your code: ImageLoader and DiskStorage.

You can be certain that ImageLoader doesn't introduce any concurrency issues, since it's an actor. But what about DiskStorage? Could that type lead to concurrency issues in your global actor?

You could argue that storage belongs to ImageDatabase, which is an actor. Therefore, storage's code executes serially, and the code in DiskStorage cannot introduce data races.

That's a valid argument, but other threads, actors or functions can create their own instances of DiskStorage. In that case, the code **could be unreliable**.

One way to address this is to convert DiskStorage to an actor as well. However, since you mostly expect ImageDatabase to work with DiskStorage, making it an actor will introduce some redundant switching between actors.

What you really need, in this chapter, is to guarantee that the code in DiskStorage always runs on ImageDatabase's serial executor. This will eliminate concurrency issues and avoid excessive **actor hopping**.

ImageDatabase executor

To do this, open **DiskStorage.swift** and prepend the class declaration with @ImageDatabase, like this:

```
@ImageDatabase class DiskStorage {
```

Instead of DiskStorage's individual methods, you move the whole type to the ImageDatabase serial executor. This way, ImageDatabase and DiskStorage can never step on each other's toes.

That wasn't difficult at all, but you now face an error:

```
Call to global actor 'ImageDatabase'-isolated initializer
'init()' in a synchronous actor-isolated context
```

The Swift compiler's complaint is valid. You cannot create DiskStorage, which runs on ImageDatabase's serial executor, *before* you've created ImageDatabase itself.

You'll fix that by deferring the storage initialization to a new method called setUp(), along with a few other things you need to take care of when you initialize your database.

Initializing the Database Actor

First, switch back to **ImageDatabase.swift**. Then, replace:

```
private let storage = DiskStorage()
```

With:

```
private var storage: DiskStorage!
```

Next, you'll add `setUp()`. Add the new method anywhere inside `ImageDatabase`:

```
func setUp() async throws {
  storage = await DiskStorage()
  for fileURL in try await storage.persistedFiles() {
    storedImagesIndex.insert(fileURL.lastPathComponent)
  }
}
```

`setUp()` initializes `DiskStorage` and reads all the files persisted on disk into the `storedImagesIndex` lookup index. Any time you save new files to disk, you'll also update the index.

You'll need to ensure you call it before any other method in `ImageDatabase`, because you'll initialize your storage there. Don't worry about this for now, though. You'll take care of it in a moment.

Writing Files to Disk

The new cache will need to write images to disk. When you fetch an image, you'll export it to PNG format and save it. To do that, add the following method anywhere inside `ImageDatabase`:

```
func store(image: UIImage, forKey key: String) async throws {
  guard let data = image.pngData() else {
    throw "Could not save image \(key)"
  }
  let fileName = DiskStorage.fileName(for: key)
  try await storage.write(data, name: fileName)
  storedImagesIndex.insert(fileName)
}
```

Here, you get the image's PNG data and save it by using the `write(_:name:)` storage method. If that goes through successfully, you add the asset to the lookup index, too.

You now face a new compiler error. To fix it, open **DiskStorage.swift** and scroll to `fileName(for:)`.

Give the method a close inspection. It looks like this is a pure function that uses no state at all, so you can safely make it **non-isolated**, as you did for similar methods in the last chapter.

Prepend `nonisolated` to the method definition, like this:

```
nonisolated static func fileName(for path: String) -> String {
```

This clears the error and lets you move on.

Fetching Images from Disk (or Elsewhere)

Next, you'll add a helper method to fetch an image from the database. If the file is already stored on disk, you'll fetch it from there. Otherwise, you'll use `ImageLoader` to make a request to the server. This is how the completed flow will look:

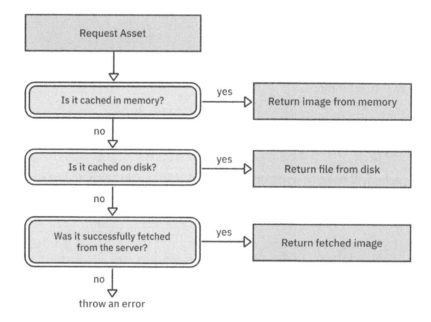

To implement this, add the initial code of the new method to `ImageDatabase`:

```
func image(_ key: String) async throws -> UIImage {
  let keys = await imageLoader.cache.keys
  if keys.contains(key) {
    print("Cached in-memory")
    return try await imageLoader.image(key)
  }

}
```

This method takes a path to an asset and either returns an image or throws an error. Before trying the disk or the network, you check if you find a cached image in memory; if so, you can get it directly from `ImageLoader.cache`.

> **Note**: Calling `contains(_:)` on the cache keys directly, without fetching a local copy of the keys collection, produces memory corruption in release builds when there are concurrent updates. That's why here you safely get a local copy of the keys and then you check for the existence of key.

Because your caching strategy is getting more complex, you also add a new log message that lets you know you've successfully retrieved an in-memory image.

In case there's no cached asset in memory, you check the on-disk index and, if there's a match, you read the file and return it.

You'll now add the rest of the logic for querying the local image database for a cached asset, as well as falling back to fetching from the remote server if one doesn't exist.

Append the following to the same method:

```
do {
  // 1
  let fileName = DiskStorage.fileName(for: key)
  if !storedImagesIndex.contains(fileName) {
    throw "Image not persisted"
  }

  // 2
  let data = try await storage.read(name: fileName)
  guard let image = UIImage(data: data) else {
    throw "Invalid image data"
  }

  print("Cached on disk")
  // 3
  await imageLoader.add(image, forKey: key)
  return image
} catch {
  // 4
}
```

This block of code is a little longer, so look at it step-by-step:

1. You get the asset file name from `DiskStorage.fileName(for:)` and check the database index for a match. If the key doesn't exist, you throw an error that transfers the execution to the `catch` statement. You'll try fetching the asset from the server there.

2. You then try reading the file from disk and initializing a `UIImage` with its contents. Again, if either of these steps fails, you throw and try to get the image from the server in the `catch` block.

3. Finally, if you successfully retrieved the cached image, you store it in memory in `ImageLoader`. This prevents you from having to make the trip to the file system and back next time.

4. In the empty `catch` block, you'll fetch the asset from the server.

To complete the method, insert this code inside `catch`:

```
let image = try await imageLoader.image(key)
try await store(image: image, forKey: key)
return image
```

This code will run if all other local attempts fail and you have to make a network call to the server. You call `ImageLoader.image(_:)` to fetch the image and, before returning, store it on disk for future use.

With that, the persistence layer is almost ready. To complete it, you'll add one final method for debugging purposes, just as you did for the image loader.

Purging the Cache

To easily test the caching logic, you'll add one more method to `ImageDatabase`. `clear()` will delete all the asset files on disk and empty the index. Add the following anywhere in `ImageDatabase`:

```
func clear() async {
  for name in storedImagesIndex {
    try? await storage.remove(name: name)
  }
  storedImagesIndex.removeAll()
}
```

Here, you iterate over all the indexed files in `storedImagesIndex` and try to delete the matching files on disk. Finally, you remove all values from the index as well.

The cache is ready; it's time to use it in EmojiArt.

Wiring up the Persistence Layer

As noted earlier, before you do anything with the new database type, you need to set it up safely by calling `ImageDatabase`'s `setUp` method. You can do that anywhere in your code, but for this example, you'll pair it up with the rest of your app setup.

Open **LoadingView.swift** and scroll to `task(...)`.

The first thing you currently do in the app is to call `model.loadImages()` in that task modifier. Insert the following **before** the line that calls `loadImages()`:

```
try await ImageDatabase.shared.setUp()
```

With that wrinkle out of the way, your next step is to replace all the current calls to `ImageLoader` with `ImageDatabase`, instead.

Once you do this, you'll always make requests to `ImageDatabase`, which serializes the access and transparently uses the image loader when an image isn't cached locally. There are, all in all, only two occurrences you need to replace.

First, open **ThumbImage.swift** and replace `imageLoader.image(file.url)` inside the `task(...)` modifier with:

```
ImageDatabase.shared.image(file.url)
```

That will check the in-memory cache, then the on-disk cache and then, if all else fails, the network.

The completed `task` code should now look like this:

```
.task {
  guard let image = try? await
    ImageDatabase.shared.image(file.url) else {
    overlay = "camera.metering.unknown"
    return
  }
  updateImage(image)
}
```

You can also delete the `imageLoader` property, since you're not using it anymore.

Secondly, open **DetailsView.swift** and replace imageLoader.image(file.url) with:

```
ImageDatabase.shared.image(file.url)
```

Delete imageLoader here, as well.

Build and run. Direct your attention to the output console; you'll see a healthy mix of network requests and assets cached in memory, like so:

```
Download: http://localhost:8080/gallery/image?26
Cached in-memory
Cached in-memory
Download: http://localhost:8080/gallery/image?2
Cached in-memory
Download: http://localhost:8080/gallery/image?9
Download: http://localhost:8080/gallery/image?22
...
```

Without losing sight of the output console, scroll all the way to the bottom of the image feed, then scroll back to the top. Once you've downloaded all the images, you'll only see memory hits like this:

```
Cached in-memory
Cached in-memory
Cached in-memory
Cached in-memory
Cached in-memory
Cached in-memory
Cached in-memory
```

So far, so good! This is exactly how your pair of star actors should behave.

Now, for the ultimate test: Stop the app and run it again. Don't scroll the feed just yet!

This time, the disk cache serves all the content without you having to fetch it from the network:

```
Cached on disk
Cached on disk
Download: http://localhost:8080/gallery/image?10
Cached on disk
Cached on disk
```

Every now and again, you'll see a network request go through; these are the assets that failed to download on the last run of the app. You retry fetching those because they're not persisted on disk.

Scroll down to the bottom and up again. You'll see that after loading all the assets from disk, the log again fills up with messages for memory-cached assets.

Congratulations, it seems like all the pieces of the jigsaw puzzle have come together to create a super-powerful image caching mechanism for your project.

No time to spend gloating, though; you have a few more tasks to complete before wrapping up.

Adding a Cache Hit Counter

In this section, you'll add code to activate the bottom bar in the feed screen to help you debug your caching mechanism. This is how the toolbar will look when you finish:

The toolbar consists of two buttons on the left side: one to clear the disk cache and one to clear the in-memory cache. On the right side, there's a cache hit counter that shows you how many assets you loaded from disk and how many from memory.

Right now, the toolbar doesn't do anything or show any real information. You'll work on it in this section.

First, you need to add a way for ImageLoader to continuously publish the count of cache hits. And, you guessed it, that sounds like a case for AsyncStream!

Open **ImageLoader.swift** and add these new properties:

```
@MainActor private(set) var inMemoryAccess: AsyncStream<Int>?

private var inMemoryAccessContinuation:
AsyncStream<Int>.Continuation?
private var inMemoryAccessCounter = 0 {
  didSet
{ inMemoryAccessContinuation?.yield(inMemoryAccessCounter) }
}
```

Here, you add a new asynchronous stream called `inMemoryAccess` that runs on the main actor. Your views can access and subscribe to this property without worrying about any background UI updates.

Additionally, you protect the current count in `inMemoryAccessCounter`, by leveraging `ImageLoader`'s actor semantics. You'll store the stream continuation in `inMemoryAccessContinuation` so you can easily produce ongoing updates. Finally, the `didSet` accessor ensures that any updates to `inMemoryAccessCounter` are relayed to the continuation, if one exists.

To correctly initialize the stream, you'll add `setUp()` to `ImageLoader`, as you previously did for your other actor. Insert the following anywhere inside the type:

```
func setUp() async {
  let accessStream = AsyncStream<Int> { continuation in
    inMemoryAccessContinuation = continuation
  }
  await MainActor.run { inMemoryAccess = accessStream }
}
```

In `setUp()`, you create a new `AsyncStream` and store its continuation in `inMemoryAccessContinuation`. Then, switching to the main actor, you store the stream itself in `inMemoryAccess`.

With this setup, you can produce new values at any given time by calling `inMemoryAccessContinuation.yield(...)`. To do that, scroll to `image(_:)` and find this case: `case .completed(let image)`. Insert this code on the next line, before the `return` statement:

```
inMemoryAccessCounter += 1
```

Here, you increase the hit counter, which in return yields the result to the stored continuation. Since both properties are on the actor, you perform both operations synchronously. However, the @MainActor annotation causes the stream to produce the value on the main actor asynchronously:

As a good developer, you'll also add a deinitializer to manually complete the stream when the actor is released from memory:

```
deinit {
    inMemoryAccessContinuation?.finish()
}
```

Displaying the Counter

You'll get around to updating your view code in a moment, but don't forget that the image loader will not set itself up automatically. You'll now add the call to ImageLoader.setUp(), just like you did for ImageDatabase.

A safe place to call ImageLoader.setUp() is your database's own setUp(). Open **ImageDatabase.swift** and find setUp(). Append the following to the bottom of the method:

```
await imageLoader.setUp()
```

With that out of the way, you can move on to updating the UI code that displays the debugging toolbar at the bottom of the image feed.

Open **BottomToolbar.swift**; add a new `task` modifier after the last `padding` in the code:

```
.task {
  guard let memoryAccessSequence =
    ImageDatabase.shared.imageLoader.inMemoryAccess else {
    return
  }
  for await count in memoryAccessSequence {
    inMemoryAccessCount = count
  }
}
```

Above, you unwrap the optional stream and use a `for await` loop to asynchronously iterate over the sequence.

Each time the stream produces a value, you assign it to `inMemoryAccessCount` — a state property on the toolbar view that you use to display the text in the toolbar.

Build and run again. Scroll up and down a little, and you'll see the in-memory counter give you updates in real-time:

Purging the in-memory cache

To complete the last exercise for this chapter, you'll wire up the button that clears the memory cache.

First, you'll add a new method to `ImageLoader` to purge the in-memory assets. Then, you'll wire up the toolbar button.

Open **ImageDatabase.swift** and add this new method that encapsulates clearing the image loader cache:

```
func clearInMemoryAssets() async {
  await imageLoader.clear()
}
```

Then switch back to **BottomToolbar.swift** and find the comment that reads `//
Clear in-memory cache`.

This code is for the right button in the toolbar. Replace the comment with the actual code to clear the memory cache:

```
Task {
  await ImageDatabase.shared.clearInMemoryAssets()
  try await model.loadImages()
}
```

In the code above, you first clear the in-memory cache, then reload the images from the server.

Build and run. Tap the button to check that the app correctly clears the memory, then gets all the assets from the network once again.

Now that you've completed that last feature, the EmojiArt app is complete. You've done a fantastic job working through all the steps in this chapter.

Feel free to jump over to the next chapter if you're eager to move on to the next topic: **distributed actors**. If you'd like to work on EmojiArt a bit longer, stay for this chapter's challenge.

Challenges

Challenge: Updating the number of Disk Fetches

In this challenge, you'll finish the debugging toolbar by connecting the second counter, which displays on-disk cache hits.

Your approach should be similar to what you did in the last section of the chapter for the in-memory counter; it shouldn't take you long.

In your implementation, follow these general steps, mirroring what you did for `ImageLoader`:

- Add an async stream for the counter to `ImageDatabase`.

- Set up the stream in the actor's `setUp()`.

- Complete the stream in a deinitializer.

- Increment the counter when you have an actual disk cache hit.

- Finally, update the toolbar view to iterate over the stream and make the last toolbar button clear the disk cache.

After you've finished working through these steps, the toolbar will be an excellent debugging tool to verify and test your caching logic:

Key Points

- **Global actors** protect the global mutable state within your app.

- Use **@globalActor** to annotate an actor as global and make it conform to the GlobalActor protocol.

- Use a global actor's **serial executor** to form concurrency-safe silos out of code that needs to work with the same mutable state.

- Use a mix of **actors** and **global actors**, along with **async/await** and **asynchronous sequences**, to make your concurrent code safe.

By completing the EmojiArt project, you've gained a solid understanding of the problems that actors solve and how to use these fancy APIs to write solid and safe concurrent code.

However, there's still one kind of actor you haven't tried yet. **Distributed actors** are, in fact, *so bleeding-edge* that the complete infrastructure to run a distributed actor system is still semi-officially released by Apple. If that sounds like a cool challenge, turn the page to the next and final chapter of this book.

Chapter 10: Actors in a Distributed System

By Marin Todorov

In the previous chapters, you learned how to run concurrent tasks in parallel on multiple CPU cores. Furthermore, you learned how to use `actor` types to make concurrency safe. In this last chapter of the book, you'll cover the advanced topic of **distributed actors**: actors that run locally as well as in *other processes* — or even on different machines altogether.

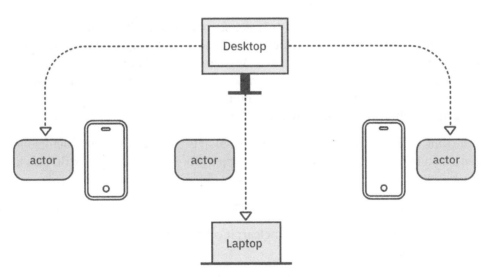

There are multiple reasons you'd want to make use of distributed actors, for example:

- To run code in a child process on the same machine. This way, if a fatal error crashes the child process, your main process will continue working and can even start a new copy of the child.

- To run a process on a remote machine, like a database server. This way, you don't need to use REST or GraphQL to send and receive data. You simply call methods directly on objects running on the server.

- Finally, you can use a cluster of devices to perform many tasks as an ensemble.

The distributed actors model has been around for some time, and libraries offer actors and distributed actors for many languages. Therefore, this chapter includes only a minimal amount of theory that covers the model in general.

Understanding the State of Distributed Actors in Swift

Distributed actors were part of Swift's larger set of proposals for modern concurrency. When Swift 5.5 introduced async/await initially, it did have partial experimental support for the distributed language feature, but not all implementations were complete. As the new concurrency features of async/await, tasks, groups and actors improved over a number of minor releases, the distributed actors did not, holistically speaking, land.

At the time of this writing, the latest Swift version is 5.8, and distributed actors have been around for more than a year, but the support for real-world usage still feels like a *work-in-progress* in some ways:

- The feature is still described as experimental.

- The documentation is somewhat unclear; it contains typos and still looks like a draft version.

- Generally, the guidelines are that actor systems are challenging to build, and developers shouldn't build them. However, there are yet to be any officially released systems by Apple for developers to use.

- The examples provided officially use a combination of async/await, classes, locks and notifications instead of leveraging modern concurrency in Swift.

Given all of the above, since it covers an experimental Swift feature, this chapter is also **experimental**. But it's fun!

In this chapter, you'll work on a project that includes an almost completed distributed actor system. You'll make a few changes to each key part: the network service, the actor system itself, the distributed actor, and the app that puts it all together.

In doing this, you'll understand how the network layer and the system work, which should give you a better understanding of how to use distributed actors if one day you have access to an official actor system or if you decide to build one yourself.

Work through the chapter with the understanding that the project follows the basics of Apple's examples and is, therefore, just a sample system for learning purposes.

Great work on making your way through this rather lengthy disclaimer! Now, it's time to get to it...

Evolving Local to Distributed

You're already familiar with actors; they isolate state by putting an automatic barrier between the type's synchronized internal state and when accessing the synchronized scope from "outside". That means calls from other actors are considered **outside access** and automatically made asynchronous:

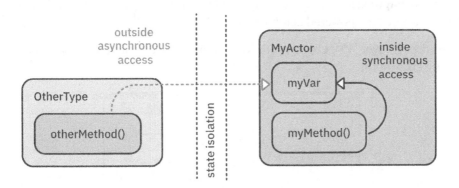

That means this process may take an arbitrary amount of time. In fact, in Chapter 6, "Testing Asynchronous Code", you had to implement a custom way to time out asynchronous calls that took longer than expected.

For local actors, the compiler transparently serializes calls that access the actor's state:

But, the compiler can sometimes inject the same logic into the isolation layer. For example, distributed actors take advantage of the isolation layer's asynchronous nature and allow you to add a **transport service** there. A transport can relay calls to actor methods to another process, to another machine on the network or to a JSON API available on a web server.

Distributed actors introduce the notion of **location transparency**, which allows you to work with both local and distributed actors in much the same way. Switching between the two requires minimal code changes.

You can choose any kind of transport because the distributed actor language feature is **transport agnostic**! The same actor could theoretically partake into a Bluetooth, REST, or websocket-powered actor system.

The transport layer sits between your local copy of the distributed actor and the one running elsewhere:

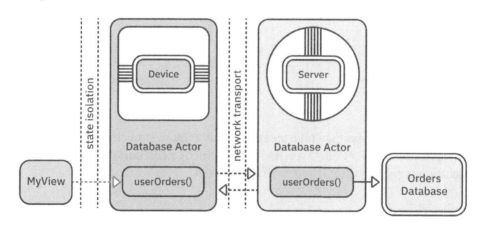

The diagram above shows an example of a local database actor that transparently forwards database queries to a server on the web. Your UI layer, MyView, uses the actor asynchronously, so it makes no difference if the actor is local or distributed.

To make writing code as straightforward as possible, distributed actors have the following constraints:

1. They allow no direct access to data from outside the actor. The model requires async method calls, allowing the transport layer to make a request and wait for a response.

2. Distributed actors are uniquely identifiable via a free-form ID property.

3. The method parameters and the method return values are automatically serialized for transport by the actor system and therefore need to conform to Codable.

4. All properties and method calls are **throwing at the point of use** to allow for transport failures. In other words, all distributed methods, even those which don't throw, should be called with try.

> **Note**: At the point of writing this, there are still wrinkles to iron out in the compiler. For example, forgetting to write a try when calling a non-throwing distributed method may simply hang the build.

Getting Started With SkyNet

In this chapter, you'll work more on the project from Chapter 7, "Concurrent Code With TaskGroup".

You won't start where you left the project at the end of Chapter 7, so make sure to open the starter project provided for *this* chapter.

You'll improve the app by adding an actor system that connects to local network devices over **Bonjour**. This will let you perform more concurrent scans using system resources across the network.

> **Note**: Bonjour is an Apple-developed network service that allows you to connect to devices on your network with no configuration: https:// en.wikipedia.org/wiki/Bonjour_(software)

The ultimate goal for this guided exercise is to scale the app's computing power by connecting more devices to a meshed network. Thus, the name of this chapter's project is **SkyNet**.

Connecting to Devices via Bonjour

At the end of Chapter 7, "Concurrent Code With TaskGroup", you completed the Sky project. The user can start a scan by tapping **Engage systems**, and the app will concurrently iterate over sectors in satellite imagery and scan them.

Open the starter project for this chapter and meet the **SkyNet** project.

SkyNet will use Bonjour to discover other iOS devices running the app and talk to them. For example, Bonjour lets you automatically find all the printers, scanners and other devices on your Wi-Fi.

As even basic networking requires a lot of boilerplate, the starter project already includes the bare bones of a functioning transport service over Bonjour.

Open **BonjourService.swift** from the **BonjourTransport** folder and peek inside.

BonjourService creates a Bonjour network session, starts an advertiser service that tells other devices about the current system and starts a browser that finds other systems on the network:

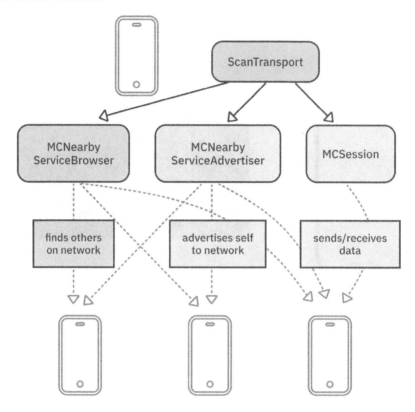

In effect, the included code automatically connects all the SkyNet devices to one other.

You'll work on BonjourService a little later to get a sense of what's happening in that type.

It's time to get coding! In this chapter, you'll work on all of the architectural layers to get a sense of them.

By the time you're done, SkyNet will be able to take over other devices and run a theoretically unlimited amount of concurrent tasks.

Creating a Distributed Actor

Firstly, you'll explore the distributed keyword. You prefix an actor, property or method with distributed to indicate that these might be invoked remotely.

Create a new Swift file called **ScanActor.swift** in the **Tasks** folder and add an empty distributed actor inside:

```
import Foundation
import Distributed

distributed actor ScanActor {
  typealias ActorSystem = BonjourActorSystem

}
```

First, you import the Distributed framework. Technically speaking, distributed actors are part of Swift itself and shouldn't require importing any frameworks. It is, however, tightly coupled with some of the types and protocols found in the Distributed framework, so you often need to import it too.

Another novelty in the code above is the distributed keyword preceding actor. Adding that new keyword turns an actor into a distributed actor; it imposes the compile-time constraints we covered earlier, adds some magic properties and methods and adds distributed behavior at runtime.

Finally, you set the distributed actor's system type to BonjourActorSystem. This is the actor system you'll use in this project, and you'll work on it in the next chapter section.

For now, add some code to the empty ScanActor type; insert:

```
private let nameValue: String

init(name: String, actorSystem: ActorSystem) {
  self.nameValue = name
  self.actorSystem = actorSystem
}
```

You add a name to the actor and set it upon initialization. This name will be the uniquely identifying ID for that actor.

You also initialize the actorSystem property, which is automagically added to the type behind the scenes for you.

Next, you'll add some remotely accessible states. Insert the following properties in
`ScanActor`:

```
distributed var name: String {
  nameValue
}

private var countValue = 0
distributed var count: Int {
  countValue
}
```

name and `count` are distributed properties, meaning you can access them remotely.
The compiler imposes the restriction of computing these properties. This is why both
of them proxy a private property in the code above.

`count` is the number of tasks the actor has currently committed to executing. You'll
track this count so you can balance how much load each of the devices in the
network takes and prevent some devices from overcommitting while others remain
idle.

Finally, add these two methods to balance and run tasks:

```
distributed func commit() {
  countValue += 1
}

distributed func run(_ task: ScanTask) async throws -> Data {
  defer {
    countValue -= 1
  }
  return try await task.run()
}
```

Similarly to the rest of the type's interface, these two methods are prefixed with
`distributed`, making them available for remote execution. When a remote system
calls `commit()`, count increases and "reserves" some of the actor's capacity.

`run(_)` takes a task parameter and executes it, much like the local app model
currently runs tasks.

> **Note**: If you follow a similar pattern in a production system, keep in mind that
> due to network failure, you might not balance the calls to `commit()` and
> `run(_)`, so you'll need more checks to verify the actor isn't committed but
> idling.

Your distributed actor is now complete. You learned how to expose state and remotely available methods. Before moving on to working on the actor system itself, you'll add some final touches to the Bonjour service.

Tracking Devices on the Local Network

The Bonjour service plays two key roles in network discovery. On one side, it "advertises" the current device on the network; on another, it listens for announcements from other devices. This way, effectively, each device tracks all other devices on the network:

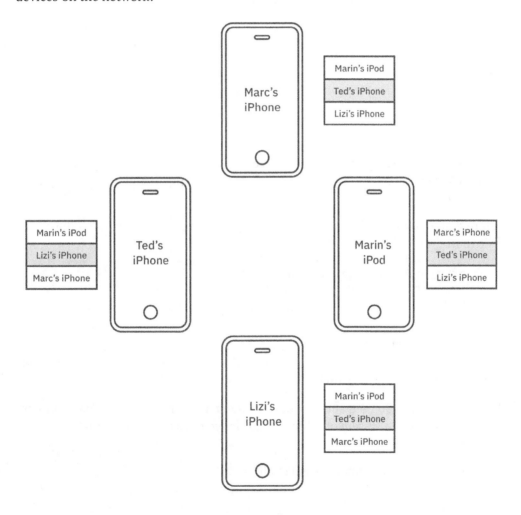

Open **BonjourService.swift** and have a look inside — whoa, there's plenty of code in there already... Most of the methods already in place are callbacks allowing Bonjour to inform you about devices getting on and off the network, errors, and so on.

To get a sense of the service, you'll alter some of the methods called when a device connects or disconnects from the local network.

Scroll down to `session(_:peer:didChange:)` and append this code at the bottom of the method:

```
if [.connected, .notConnected].contains(state) {
  actorSystem?.connectivityChangedFor(
    deviceName: peerID.displayName,
    to: state == .connected
  )
}
```

This method callback receives a device name (`peerID`) and its status, which could be `notConnected`, `connecting`, or `connected`.

If a device has disconnected or successfully connected, you'd like to notify the system so it can add or remove it from the list of available actors.

`connectivityChangedFor(deviceName:to:)` is a custom method on the `BonjourActorSystem` actor system, which is currently empty. You will implement it in a moment.

Before that, find the method called `browser(_:lostPeer:)` and add the following code to it:

```
actorSystem?.connectivityChangedFor(
  deviceName: peerID.displayName,
  to: false
)
```

This is the method that the bonjour "browser" calls if a device disappears from the network. In this case, you call the same method as before, but you set the connected status directly to `false` this time.

As you can see, the Bonjour service doesn't "understand" much about what your app is doing, it's mostly a system of callbacks that let you react to changes on the network.

Next, you'll work on the actor system itself.

Managing Actors in a Distributed System

An actor system may take on many tasks; using or managing a data transport such as Bluetooth, encode and decode invocations across the wire, manage a list of available remote actors, receive remote requests and many others.

Generally speaking, a system should be able to at least send requests and receive responses to allow you to access remote actor properties or methods:

Essentially, the actor system's main purpose is to automate all the steps you would usually implement manually when adding networking to your app. It tracks connected actors that your local device can reach out to, and when they need to send and receive messages, it encodes all the data for transporting and decode it at the receiving side.

If you have a well-designed system, you'll ideally never bother making a network call manually again.

In this chapter, you will only delve into some of the details of implementing a system; you'll only scratch the surface by completing a couple of missing features in the starter code. Feel free to read through the rest and learn further from Apple's `Distributed` framework documentation.

Firstly, your system needs to track the local actor for the current device, so it knows when to retry tasks that fail to execute remotely.

Open **BonjourActorSystem.swift** and add this new property in `BonjourActorSystem`:

```
var localActor: ScanActor!
```

Then, append the code to initialize the local actor at the end of `init(localName: String)`:

```
self.localActor = ScanActor(
  name: localName,
  actorSystem: self
)

withActors { $0[localActor.id] = localActor }
```

The first line of code creates a `ScanActor` instance with the local device name as an ID. Then, you use the `withActors(_)` function that gives you thread-safe access to the system's `actors` dictionary and adds the local one.

> **Note**: `withActors(_)` uses a lock to guarantee safe access to the list of actors, similar to Apple's examples.

Now that you have the local actor safe and sound, you can move on to track the rest of the actors in the system. Scroll down to `connectivityChangedFor(deviceName:to:)` and add the options to add and remove actors.

First, append:

```
if connected {
  if let remoteActor = try? ScanActor
    .resolve(id: name, using: self) {
    withActors { $0[remoteActor.id] = remoteActor }
  }
}
```

`resolve(id:using:)` is another method automagically added to your actors by the compiler without you having to adopt a protocol or implement yourself. It's a factory method that, given an identifier and an actor system, creates an instance of your actor type.

When the device has connected, and you have resolved the remote actor, you add it to the list of system actors.

Now, add at the bottom of the method:

```
else {
  withActors { $0.removeValue(forKey: name) }
  NotificationCenter.default.post(
    name: .disconnected, object: name
  )
}
```

Besides removing the remote actor for the given ID, you also send a notification. The actor system listens for `.disconnect` notifications to cancel network requests if the receiver device has just disconnected.

Now it's time to finally run the app. First, build and run the project in a simulator of your choice.

There's a good chance that the first thing you'll notice is a macOS system alert that asks permission for Sky.app to talk to other devices over the local network:

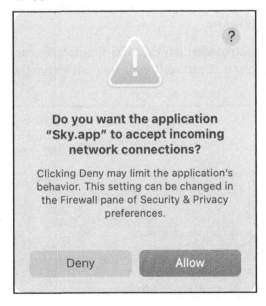

If you see this dialog, click **Allow** to give SkyNet access to the network; that will take you to the app's main screen:

You don't see much difference from how the app looked at the end of Chapter 7, "Concurrent Code With TaskGroup", do you?

Of course not, at this point, SkyNet is only running on a *single* device. This is not SkyNet, it's just the Sky project. Tap the **Engage systems** button; you'll see that the app works just as it did before.

Luckily, Xcode allows you to start multiple iOS simulators simultaneously! While you're running the project, select a different simulator from the device list next to the scheme selector:

Once you start the app on a second or a third simulator, Xcode will stop the app on the previously running simulator. You'll need to manually restart SkyNet on the simulator(s) so you can have a few copies of the app working together.

> **Note**: If you have an older Mac, it might not be happy running multiple simulators simultaneously, and it might not be able to devote multiple cores to multiple simulators. In that case, you'll need to run at least one copy of the app on a device to see the best results.

As soon as you launch the project on your additional device, a connectivity icon will appear in the top-right corner:

If you tap the icon, you'll see a list of all the connected devices.

Note that the connectivity framework is quite verbose. The output console fills up quickly with messages along the lines of:

```
[MCNearbyDiscoveryPeerConnection] Read failed.
[MCNearbyDiscoveryPeerConnection] Stream error occurred: Code=54
"Connection reset by peer"
Connectivity: iPhone SE (3rd generation) true
[GCKSession] Failed to send a DTLS packet with 117 bytes;
sendmsg error: No route to host (65).
[GCKSession] Something is terribly wrong; no clist for remoteID
[1104778395] channelID [-1].
...
```

For the most part, you can ignore these messages. They make looking for your own logs a little difficult, but the connectivity framework usually quiets down after a few moments.

Before wrapping up this section, you'll add one more method to find the first available actor whenever you need to execute a task remotely.

Since the system keeps a list of all actors and each actor keeps track of the tasks it's currently committed to running, it should be simple enough to loop over the list and find the first actor with some availability.

Add the new method to `BonjourActorSystem`:

```
func firstAvailableActor() async throws
  -> ScanActor {
  while true {

  }
  fatalError("Will never execute")
}
```

This method will return an actor or throw and, therefore, never reach that one last line, throwing a fatal error. You do need it to satisfy the compiler's desire that all code paths correctly wrap up the method execution.

The `while` loop ensures you'll keep trying to find an actor until there is an available one.

Next, insert the following code inside the `while` to loop over the system's actors:

```
for nextID in withActors(\.keys) {

}
try await Task.sleep(for: .milliseconds(100))
```

This code takes the identifiers of all actors and, in the for body, will probe each in turn to find the first that has free capacity.

Just in case you loop over all actors and none have the capacity, you wait for a moment, about 100 milliseconds, before restarting the loop.

Finally, insert inside the code to inspect each actor inside the for loop:

```
guard let nextActor = try? ScanActor
  .resolve(id: nextID, using: self),
  await nextActor.count < 4 else {
    continue
}

do {
  try await nextActor.commit()
  return nextActor
} catch { }
```

As you did previously, you try to resolve the actor, and if that succeeds, you verify that the actor hasn't already committed to executing four or more tasks.

Ultimately, if you find a match, you call commit() on the actor and return it as a result. This "reserves" some of the actor's capacity, as per your code in ScanActor.commit(), and you're ready to send a scan task to the returned actor.

Don't get spooked by the empty catch in the code block. Since commit() itself is not throwing, the only way for that call to throw is if the network fails. In that case, you just swallow the error and let the for loop continue so you can try the next actor.

With these last changes, all of the chess pieces are set on the board, and with a few swift moves, you need to swap the old code with the new code to get everything working.

Using a System Instead of a Single Actor

In this section, you'll leave behind the service and the actor system and move on to updating the app model.

Open **ScanModel.swift** and scroll down to the worker(number:) method.

You likely remember from Chapter 7, "Concurrent Code With TaskGroup" that worker(number:) takes the input for a scan task, creates it and runs it.

In this section, you'll adjust the method to forward the task to an actor instead of always running it locally.

Firstly, add a second parameter to the method called `actor` like so:

```
func worker(number: Int, actor: ScanActor) async
-> Result<Data, Error> {
```

Then replace the line `result = try .success(await task.run())` with:

```
result = try .success(await actor.run(task))
```

Nice! This is all you need to do to move the work from your local system to execute across devices over the local network potentially. You do, however, face an error right now, and there's no time like the present to take care of it.

Since `runAllTasks()` will work quite differently than before, go ahead and remove all the code inside that method. Next, you'll re-add some of the code and sprinkle in some new goodness as well.

First of all, re-add the basic group code:

```
started = Date()
try await withThrowingTaskGroup(
  of: Result<Data, Error>.self
) { [unowned self] group in

}
```

You'll insert code inside the group closure in the rest of this section.

You'll add as many tasks to the group as the `total` amount is set to. However, and this is important, since `firstAvailableActor()` suspends until it finds a free actor, you'll never create more tasks than your system can currently handle.

Insert this code inside the group closure from above:

```
for number in 0 ..< total {
  let actor = try await
    actorSystem.firstAvailableActor()

  group.addTask {
    return await self.worker(
      number: number,
      actor: actor
    )
  }
}
```

For each planned task, you find the first available actor. While the local system has capacity, that's always the local actor. Then you add a concurrent task that executes the work on the given actor.

Next, just as before, you'll loop over the completed tasks and print the results. Append, still in the group body:

```
for try await result in group {
  switch result {
  case .success(let result):
    print("Completed: \(result)")
  case .failure(let error):
    print("Failed: \(error.localizedDescription)")
  }
}
```

And finally, once you have processed all the results, you should reset the stats. Append to the group closure directly after the last code inserted:

```
await MainActor.run {
  completed = 0
  countPerSecond = 0
  scheduled = 0
  counted = 0
}
print("Done.")
```

Build and run the project on two or more simulators and tap **Engage Systems** in one of the running apps while having the app running in all of them. This should start the system and leverage the actors in each device. Ultimately, you should see reduced duration when the work completes:

A single device needed just over 20 seconds to complete the work but running SkyNet in two simulators gets the work done in about half the time!

Now, imagine how powerful your iPhone could become if it could spawn an actor system using all the idle CPUs on your home WIFI — your vacuum robot, smart watches, all the phones, your routers and printers! You just have to check which of those devices run Swift and get busy coding...

Updating the UI to Showcase Collaborative Work

While it's pretty impressive to make simulators join SkyNet and work together, presentation is important, too. Right now, collaborating on the search for alien life seems a little...unspectacular.

Before moving on to the last few heavy-duty tasks in this chapter, you'll include a little animation onscreen when devices connect and start a joint scan session. The starter project already includes the animation, so you just need to set a flag to `true` when performing joint work.

Open **ScanModel.swift** and add a `didSet` handler to the `scheduled` property, so it looks like this:

```
@MainActor @Published var scheduled = 0 {
  didSet {
    Task {
      isCollaborating = scheduled > 0
        && actorSystem.actorCount > 1
    }
  }
}
```

The starter project UI code will pick up `isCollaborating`'s value change and then play an animation onscreen while the property is set to `true`.

Build and run on all the iOS Simulators you're currently testing on. Then, tap **Engage systems** on one of the devices and enjoy the cool logo animation.

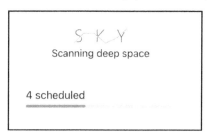

Your UI has really come alive! A connection indicator shows when devices connect, and a cool animation tells the user when the app is doing heavy work across nodes in SkyNet.

Now it's time to make things really neat. Adding a bit of code to make those other remote devices display an animation when they run errands for the actor system initiating the work.

To reassure yourself that it is actually working on remote devices, you'll also add some logging messages.

Open **ScanActor.swift** and append to `commit()`:

```
NotificationCenter.default.post(
  name: .localTaskUpdate,
  object: nil,
  userInfo: [Notification.taskStatusKey: "Committed"]
)
```

The `.localTaskUpdate` notification tells the model that something has changed relating to local tasks, and the UI should be updated. The user info dictionary of the notification contains a status message which'll be displayed at the bottom of the screen.

The other method where you change the status of running tasks is `run(_:)`, so move over to that method.

At the beginning of `run(_:)`, create an empty dictionary for the notification:

```
var info: [String: Any] = [:]
```

Now, add the following code to the end of the `defer` block:

```
NotificationCenter.default.post(
  name: .localTaskUpdate,
  object: nil,
  userInfo: info
)
```

This will post the notification once the task is complete.

Then, populate the dictionary based on the results of the task. Replace the `return` statement with the following code:

```
do {
  let data = try await task.run()
  info[Notification.taskStatusKey] = "Task \(task.input)
```

```
Completed"
    return data
} catch {
    info[Notification.taskStatusKey] = "Task \(task.input) Failed"
    throw error
}
```

This code will add the correct message to the user info dictionary.

Finally, you need to listen for the `.localTaskUpdate` notification and update the view accordingly.

Open **ScanModel.swift** and append a second task to the body of `systemConnectivityHandler()`:

```
Task {
    for await notification in NotificationCenter.default
        .notifications(named: .localTaskUpdate) {
        let status = notification.taskStatus
        let runningTasksCount = try await
actorSystem.localActor.count
        Task { @MainActor in
            if scheduled == 0 {
                isCollaborating = runningTasksCount > 0
            }
            localTasksCompleted.append(status)
        }
    }
}
```

In this code, you asynchronously loop over any `.localTaskUpdate` notifications. On each update, you check if there aren't locally scheduled tasks, but the actor is running tasks — when this condition is met, it means the actor is running tasks sent over the network. You also add the status message to the log.

> **Note**: At the time of writing, Xcode 14.2 incorrectly shows a warning that you're using `try` to access a non-throwing property in that code. Following the warning message and removing the `try` would hang the compiler.

Like you did previously, make sure to build and run the project on two or more simulators. Then start all the copies of SkyNet and tap Engage Systems in one of them. You'll see the devices that receive a task to run their logo animation and confirmation of which device is running which task will appear in the logs.

Retrying Failed Tasks

While it might seem like you're finished with this chapter, there's one final task to take care of.

You've probably noticed that thanks to the code you added in Chapter 7, "Concurrent Code With TaskGroup", you skip over any failed tasks and never return to them.

The code in **ScanTask.swift** calls `UnreliableAPI.action(failingEvery:)` to fail every tenth task so you can verify your error-handling skills. You catch the error when the local system fails and print a log message. When one of the remote systems fails to run the task, your request simply times out.

To wrap up SkyNet, you'll add new logic to retry failed tasks. After all, you don't want to miss any signs of alien life because one of the scans failed on the first try, do you?

Open **ScanModel.swift** and scroll to `runAllTasks()`. Here, you'll run your concurrent task group and expect each task to return a `Result<String, Error>`. `Result` helps you gracefully handle errors. You'll use the `Result.failure` case to print the error message to the output.

To retry failed tasks, you won't need the error; however, you will need the task itself. To handle that, you'll add your own custom error type. Add the following anywhere inside `ScanModel`:

```
struct ScanTaskError: Error {
  let underlyingError: Error
  let task: ScanTask
}
```

This is especially useful for remotely executed tasks, which can fail for many reasons: shaky connections, timeouts, etc.

Back in `runAllTasks()`, replace `Result<Data, Error>.self` with `Result<Data, ScanTaskError>.self`. This causes a few compile errors.

Scroll to `worker(number:actor:)` and change its return type from `Result<Data, Error>` to:

```
Result<Data, ScanTaskError>
```

Then, towards the middle of the method body, replace the line that defines the result variable with:

```
let result: Result<Data, ScanTaskError>
```

Finally, in that same method, replace result = .failure(error) with:

```
result = .failure(.init(
  underlyingError: error,
  task: task
))
```

That takes care of the updates in worker(...).

Next, scroll to your current error handling code in runAllTasks():

```
case .failure(let error):
  print("Failed: \(error.localizedDescription)")
```

Here, you'll get the failed task and schedule it to execute on the local system once again. Replace the current case with:

```
case .failure(let error):
  group.addTask(priority: .high) {
    print("Re-run task: \(error.task.input).")
    print("Failed with: \(error.underlyingError)")
    return await self.worker(
      number: error.task.input,
      actor: self.actorSystem.localActor
    )
  }
```

This addition will ensure that, if one task fails, whether remote or local, you add a new task to the group and retry the scan on the local system.

From experience, the best way to handle retrying tasks involves keeping track of how many times you've tried a task. It's annoying when a task always fails, but you keep retrying it indefinitely.

Luckily, SkyNet will ultimately complete all the tasks that failed initially so that the current retrying logic will suffice.

Build and run. Look at the output console:

```
Completed: 11
Completed: 9 by Marin's iPod
Re-run task: 16. Failed with:
UnreliableAPI.action(failingEvery:) failed. <---
Completed: 12
Completed: 13 by Ted's iPhone
Completed: 14 by Ted's iPhone
Completed: 17
Completed: 15
Completed: 18
Completed: 16
Re-run task: 19. Failed with:
UnreliableAPI.action(failingEvery:) failed. <---
Completed: 19
Done.
```

You see, some of the remote tasks failed, timed out, and the app ran them locally once again to complete the full scan.

You also see that the app happily reports that it worked through the full batch of tasks:

With that last addition, your work here is truly done!

Congratulations on completing this final book project. There was a lot to take care of: an actor system, networking service, distributed actors, new model logic and plenty more!

Key Points

- Systems of distributed actors communicate over a **transport layer** that can use many different underlying services: local network, Bonjour, REST service, web socket and more.

- Thanks to **location transparency**, regardless of whether the actor method calls are relayed to another process or a different machine, you use a simple `await` call at the point of use.

- In a system of distributed actors, each needs a **unique address** to relay requests reliably to the target peer and the responses delivered back to the original actor.

- Using distributed actors can fail for a myriad of reasons, so **asynchronous error handling** plays an even more significant role in such apps.

- Last but not least, a distributed app uses *the same APIs* as a local app: `async/await`, task groups and actors. The actor model allows for encapsulating the transport layer and keeping its implementation hidden from the API consumers.

Where to Go From Here?

Completing this book is no small feat!

You started in Chapter 1, "Why Modern Swift Concurrency?" by writing some of your first async/await code and some pesky asynchronous tasks. Not long after that, you were already juggling tasks, continuations and asynchronous sequences, each furthering your understanding of the new concurrency model.

In the book's second half, you moved forward with more advanced topics like testing, dynamic concurrency and — wait for it — actors. These ensure you're as concurrent as possible while avoiding some of the usual multithreading problems like data races and crashes.

By now, modern Swift concurrency should hold no secrets for you. If you have thoughts, questions or ideas you'd like to share with this book's readers, be sure to let us know in the book forums.

I want to leave you with this old proverb, which the Spider-Man comic books popularized. I think it's fitting for the last page of the book, given your newly acquired, vast knowledge of concurrent programming:

"With great power comes great responsibility."

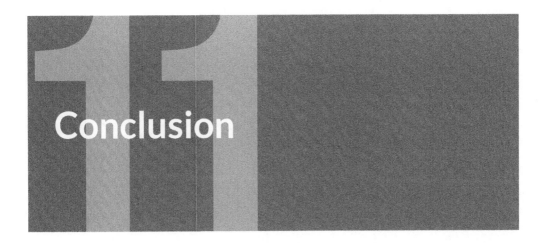

Conclusion

You've made it! You should be super proud of yourself for completing this book. Concurrency can be a challenging topic to master, but that just makes your achievement that much sweeter. With your newly acquired knowledge, you are well poised to move on to trying some of Swift's new concurrency features in the real world.

As you start incorporating async/await into your app and leveraging the powerful modern concurrency features Swift offers, like **tasks** and **actors**, your app will become safer and more predictable when it reads and mutates your data concurrently. It will also become safer to reason about, because your code will "read synchronously" but run asynchronously.

We hope the concepts you've learned in this book helped you think differently about how to plan concurrent and parallel code in the modern world, while still keeping your sanity.

If you've enjoyed learning about Swift's concurrency features, you might also enjoy our book *Combine: Asynchronous Programming with Swift*. It showcases another modern variation for modeling and composing asynchronous work.

If you have any questions or comments as you work through this book, please stop by our forums at https://forums.kodeco.com and look for the particular forum category for this book.

Thank you again for purchasing this book. Your continued support is what makes the books, tutorials, videos and other things we do at Kodeco possible. We truly appreciate it!

– The *Modern Concurrency in Swift* team

Made in the USA
Las Vegas, NV
14 February 2025

18175061R00149